#1 Teacher Recommended!

Summer Bridge
ACTIVITIES®

BRIDGING GRADES
1 to 2

Carson Dellosa Education
Greensboro, North Carolina

Caution: Exercise activities may require adult supervision. Before beginning any exercise activity, consult a physician. Written parental permission is suggested for those using this book in group situations. Children should always warm up prior to beginning any exercise activity and should stop immediately if they feel any discomfort during exercise.

Caution: Before beginning any food activity, ask parents' permission and inquire about the child's food allergies and religious or other food restrictions.

Caution: Nature activities may require adult supervision. Before beginning any nature activity, ask parents' permission and inquire about the child's plant and animal allergies. Remind the child not to touch plants or animals during the activity without adult supervision.

Caution: Before completing any balloon activity, ask parents' permission and inquire about possible latex allergies. Also, remember that uninflated or popped balloons may present a choking hazard.

The authors and publisher are not responsible or liable for any injury that may result from performing the exercises or activities in this book.

Summer Bridge®
An imprint of Carson Dellosa Education
PO Box 35665
Greensboro, NC 27425 USA

Printed in the USA • All rights reserved.   ISBN 978-1-4838-1581-7

23-071231151

Table of Contents

Making the Most of *Summer Bridge Activities* ®...iv

Skills Matrix vi

Summer Reading for Everyone viii

Summer Learning Is Everywhere! x

Section I: Monthly Goals and Word List...1

Introduction to Flexibility...2

Activity Pages 3

Science Experiments 43

Social Studies Activities...45

Outdoor Extension Activities 48

Section II: Monthly Goals and Word List 49

Introduction to Strength...50

Activity Pages 51

Science Experiments 91

Social Studies Activities...93

Outdoor Extension Activities 96

Section III: Monthly Goals and Word List..97

Introduction to Endurance...98

Activity Pages 99

Science Experiments 139

Social Studies Activities...141

Outdoor Extension Activities 144

Answer Key...145

Flash Cards

Certificate of Completion

Making the Most of *Summer Bridge Activities*®

This book will help your child review first grade skills and preview second grade skills. Inside, find lots of resources that encourage your child to practice, learn, and grow while getting a head start on the new school year.

Just 15 Minutes a Day

...is all it takes to stay sharp with learning activities for each weekday, all summer long!

Month-by-Month Organization

Three color-coded sections match the three months of summer vacation. Each month begins with a goal-setting and vocabulary-building activity. You'll also find an introduction to the section's fitness and character-building focus.

Daily Activities

Two pages of activities are provided for each weekday. They'll take about 15 minutes to complete. Activities cover math, reading comprehension, writing, grammar, and more.

Special Features

FITNESS FLASH: Quick exercises to develop strength, flexibility, and fitness

CHARACTER CHECK: Ideas for developing kindness, honesty, tolerance, and more

FACTOID: Fun trivia facts

Plenty of Bonus Features
...match your child's needs and interests!

Bonus Activities

Social studies activities explore places, maps, and more—a perfect complement to summer travel. Science experiments invite your child to interact with the world and build critical thinking skills.

Take It Outside!

A collection of fun ideas for outdoor observation, exploration, learning, and play is provided for each summer month.

Skill-Building Flash Cards

Cut out the cards at the back of the book. Store in a zip-top bag or punch a hole in each one and thread on a ring. Take the cards along with you for practice on the go.

Give a High-Five
...to your child for a job well done!

Star Stickers

Use the star stickers at the back of the book. Place a sticker in the space provided at the end of each day's learning activities when the pages are complete.

Praise and Rewards

After completing learning activities for a whole week or month, offer a reward. It could be a special treat, an outing, or time spent together. Praise the progress your child has made.

Certificate of Congratulations

At the end of the summer, complete and present the certificate at the back of the book. Congratulate your child for being well prepared for the next school year.

Skills Matrix

DAY	Addition	Fitness & Character Education	Geometry & Measurement	Graphing	Handwriting	Language Arts & Grammar	Number Relationships	Numbers & Counting	Patterning	Phonics	Place Value	Problem Solving	Reading Comprehension	Science	Social Studies	Spelling	Subtraction	Time & Money	Vocabulary	Writing
1					★					★			★							
2	★				★	★							★				★			
3						★				★								★		
4			★			★				★							★			
5	★					★				★							★			
6		★				★				★	★									
7										★	★	★								
8					★														★	★
9			★										★							
10										★			★			★	★			
11	★												★				★			
12	★					★				★							★			
13						★				★										
14	★					★							★				★			
15		★										★	★							
16						★				★			★							
17			★			★				★										
18												★	★							★
19		★	★				★						★							
20			★							★			★						★	
BONUS PAGES!														★	★					★
1	★					★	★													
2						★	★			★			★							
3	★	★								★		★					★			
4						★	★			★						★				
5				★						★			★							★
6	★	★														★	★			
7			★							★		★	★							
8										★			★						★	
9						★						★				★				★
10	★					★	★			★										
11			★			★											★			★

Skills Matrix

DAY	Addition	Fitness & Character Education	Geometry & Measurement	Graphing	Handwriting	Language Arts & Grammar	Number Relationships	Numbers & Counting	Patterning	Phonics	Place Value	Problem Solving	Reading Comprehension	Science	Social Studies	Spelling	Subtraction	Time & Money	Vocabulary	Writing
12		★											★				★	★		
13						★					★							★		
14								★		★										★
15	★					★							★				★			
16						★											★			
17	★		★			★														
18						★							★					★		
19						★							★					★		
20	★			★									★				★			★
BONUS PAGES!													★	★	★					★
1	★									★			★			★				
2			★			★										★	★			
3	★		★								★									
4								★				★	★							
5										★	★		★							★
6									★											★
7	★		★										★						★	
8		★	★									★	★							
9			★	★		★						★								
10	★																★	★		★
11	★					★													★	
12	★									★		★	★							
13													★							★
14		★							★								★			★
15	★										★		★				★			
16						★							★							
17		★					★						★			★				
18			★										★							
19						★							★				★			
20				★		★					★									
BONUS PAGES!													★	★	★					★

vii

© Carson Dellosa Education

Summer Reading for Everyone

Reading is the single most important skill for school success. Experts recommend that first and second grade students read for at least 20 minutes each day. Help your child choose several books from this list based on his or her interests. Choose at least one fiction (F) and one nonfiction (NF) title. Then, head to the local library to begin your reading adventure!

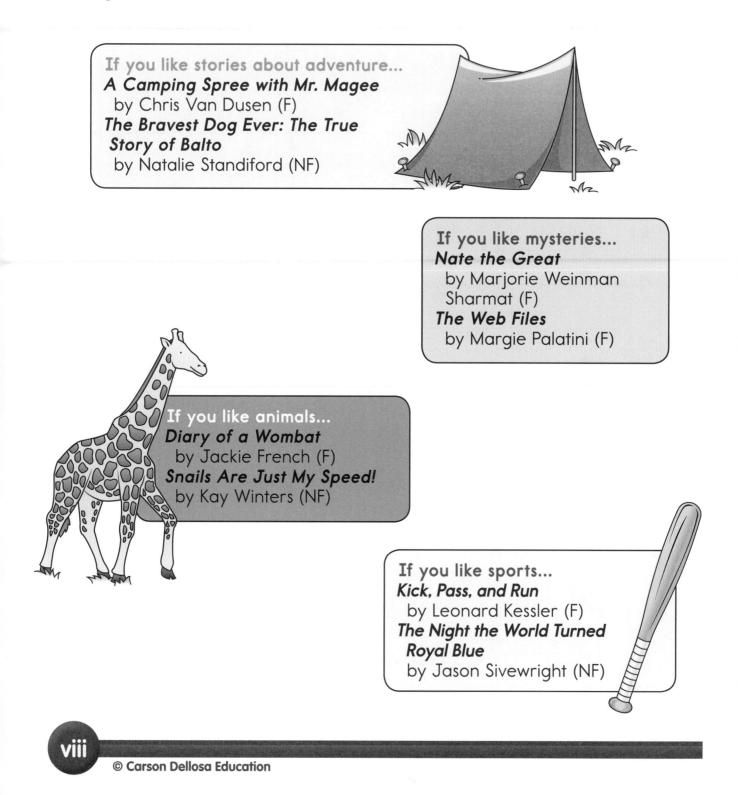

If you like stories about adventure...
A Camping Spree with Mr. Magee
   by Chris Van Dusen (F)
The Bravest Dog Ever: The True Story of Balto
   by Natalie Standiford (NF)

If you like mysteries...
Nate the Great
   by Marjorie Weinman Sharmat (F)
The Web Files
   by Margie Palatini (F)

If you like animals...
Diary of a Wombat
   by Jackie French (F)
Snails Are Just My Speed!
   by Kay Winters (NF)

If you like sports...
Kick, Pass, and Run
   by Leonard Kessler (F)
The Night the World Turned Royal Blue
   by Jason Sivewright (NF)

If you like stories about the past...
The Empty Pot
  by Demi (F)
Clara and the Shirtwaist Makers'
  Strike of 1909
  by Michelle Markel (NF)

If you like stories about communities...
The Big Umbrella
  by Amy June Bates and
  Juniper Bates (F)
Look Where We Live!
  by Scot Ritchie (NF)

If you like autobiographies...
Trombone Shorty
  by Troy Andrews (NF)
The Scraps Book: Notes from
  a Colorful Life
  by Lois Ehlert (NF)

If you like to dance...
Ella Bella Ballerina and Cinderella
  by James Mayhew (F)
You Should Meet: Misty Copeland
  by Laurie Calkhoven (NF)

If you like the ocean...
Narwhal: Unicorn of the Sea
  by Ben Clanton (F)
Manfish: A Story of Jacques
  Cousteau
  by Jennifer Berne (NF)

If you like crafts and maker projects...
Don't Let the Pigeon Finish This Activity Book!
  by Mo Willems (F)
Cardboard Creations: Open-Ended
  Exploration with Recycled Materials
  by Barbara Rucci (NF)

Summer Learning Is Everywhere!

Find learning opportunities wherever you go, all summer long!

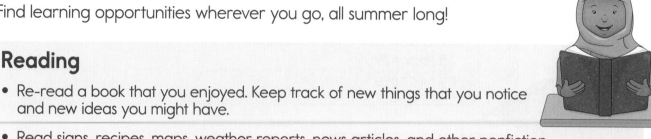

Reading

- Re-read a book that you enjoyed. Keep track of new things that you notice and new ideas you might have.

- Read signs, recipes, maps, weather reports, news articles, and other nonfiction texts that provide useful information.

Language Arts

- Trade letters, emails, or texts with a friend or relative to share summer adventures. Include stories, poems, facts, drawings, and photos.

- Pick a character from your favorite book or movie and write a letter to them.

Math

- Play math games in the car. Have each person choose an object, such as blue cars, to count; the winner has a higher number at the end of the trip. Add the numbers on license plates or compare gas prices.

- Play guessing games, such as estimating how many pieces of candy are in a jar and then counting them to see if you were right.

Science & Social Studies

- Learn about your area's history. Pick one event to explain to a friend.

- Learn about stars, the Milky Way, meteors, the moon, and other things in space. Set up blankets under the night sky and invite friends. Teach what you learned.

Character & Fitness

- Go to a concert, festival, or parade in a neighborhood that is different from yours. Tell your family members five things you enjoyed about the experience.

- Create a new dance for your favorite song. Practice it until you feel comfortable doing it without stopping.

Monthly Goals

A *goal* is something that you want to accomplish. Sometimes, reaching a goal can be hard work!

Think of three goals to set for yourself this month. For example, you may want to learn five new vocabulary words each week. Have an adult help you write your goals on the lines.

Place a sticker next to each of your goals that you complete. Feel proud that you have met your goals!

1. _____ PLACE STICKER HERE

2. _____ PLACE STICKER HERE

3. _____ PLACE STICKER HERE

Word List

The following words are used in this section. They are good words for you to know. Read each word aloud with an adult. When you see a word from this list on a page, circle it with your favorite color of crayon.

compare	question
correct	sentence
events	solve
half	title
long	true

Introduction to Flexibility

This section includes fitness and character development activities that focus on flexibility. These activities are designed to get your child moving and to get her thinking about building her physical fitness and her character. If your child has limited mobility, feel free to modify any suggested exercises to fit individual abilities.

Physical Flexibility

Flexibility, to the average person, means being able to accomplish everyday physical tasks easily, like bending to tie a shoe. These everyday tasks can be difficult for people whose muscles and joints have not been used and stretched regularly.

Proper stretching allows muscles and joints to move through their full range of motion, which is key to maintaining good flexibility. There are many ways that your child stretches every day without realizing it. She may reach for a dropped pencil or a box of cereal on the top shelf. Point out these examples to your child and explain why good flexibility is important to her health and growth. Challenge her to improve her flexibility consciously. Encourage her to set a stretching goal for the summer, such as practicing daily until she can touch her toes.

Flexibility of Character

While it is important to have a flexible body, it is also important to be mentally flexible. Share with your child that being mentally flexible means being open minded. Talk about how disappointing it can be when things do not go her way and explain how that is a normal reaction. Give a recent example of when unforeseen circumstances ruined her plans, such as having a trip to the park canceled because of rain. Explain that there will be situations in life when unforeseen things happen. Often, it is how a person reacts to those circumstances that affects the outcome. By using relatable examples, you can arm your child with tools to be flexible, such as having realistic expectations, brainstorming solutions to make a disappointing situation better, and looking for good things that may have resulted from the initial disappointment.

Mental flexibility can take many forms. For example, respecting the differences of other children, sharing, and taking turns are ways that your child can practice flexibility. Encourage your child to be flexible and praise her when you see her exhibiting this important character trait.

Read the poem.

Pitter-Patter

Pitter-patter, pitter-patter.
How I love the rain!

Storm clouds moving in,
The rain is about to begin.
How I love to see the rain!

Tiny sprinkles on my face,
Little droplets playing chase.
How I love to feel the rain!

I open up my mouth so wide,
Letting little drops inside.
How I love to taste the rain!

Tapping on my window,
It's a rhythm that I know.
How I love to hear the rain!

Everything looks so green,
And the fresh air smells so clean.
How I love to smell the rain!

Pitter-patter, pitter-patter.
How I love the rain!

Draw a line to match each sense with a detail in the poem.

	Sense	Detail
1.	sight	tapping a rhythm on the window
2.	touch	storm clouds moving in
3.	taste	little drops inside my mouth
4.	hearing	tiny sprinkles on my face
5.	smell	clean, fresh air

DAY 1

Write the capital letters of the alphabet.

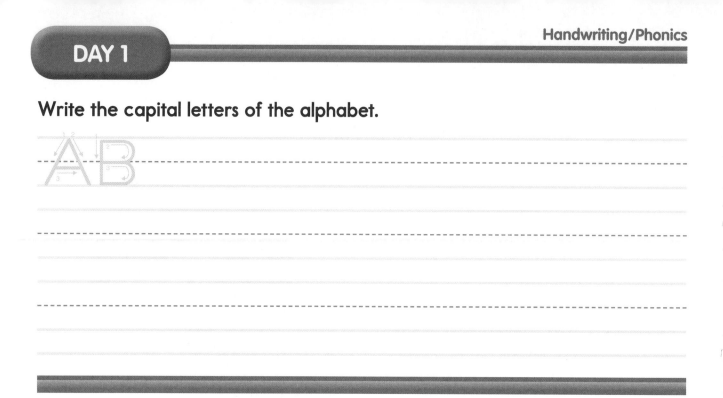

Say the name of each picture. Write the vowel that completes each word.

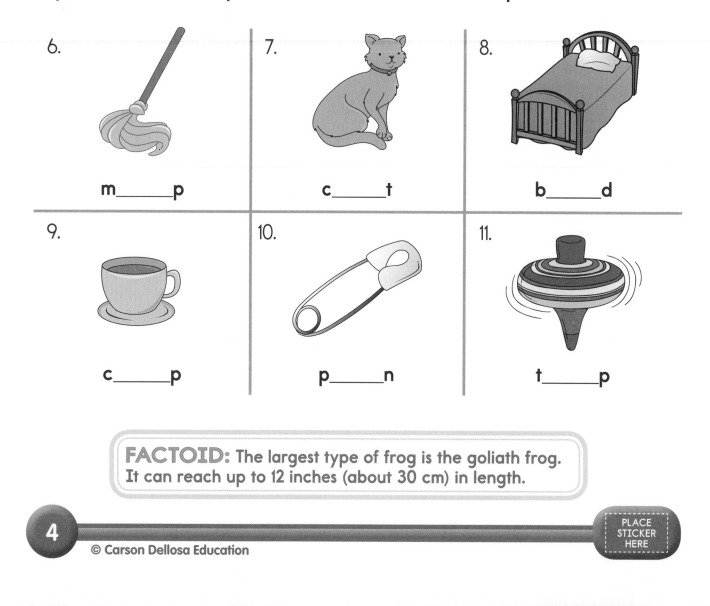

6.

m_____p

7.

c_____t

8.

b_____d

9.

c_____p

10.

p_____n

11.

t_____p

FACTOID: The largest type of frog is the goliath frog. It can reach up to 12 inches (about 30 cm) in length.

PLACE STICKER HERE

Solve each problem.

1.	2.	3.	4.	5.	6.
15 −11	16 − 4	13 − 8	13 + 5	19 − 3	18 + 2

7.	8.	9.	10.	11.	12.
8 +9	17 − 9	18 − 4	12 + 6	17 − 4	15 + 4

Rewrite each sentence below with a new verb. Look at the word in parentheses ( ) to see whether the new verb should be in the present, past, or future tense.

13. Sanja eats soup for lunch.

    (past) _____

14. Eli raced down the hill.

    (future) _____

15. Abby splashed her brother in the pool.

    (present) _____

16. The piano will need to be tuned.

    (present) _____

17. Ty will slam the car door.

    (past) _____

Write the lowercase letters of the alphabet.

a b

Read each sentence. Draw a picture of your favorite sentence.

18.   The cat sat on Alfonso's lap.

      The cat plays with the ball.

      The boy has a pet frog.

      The frog hops on Sam's bed.

      The man sat on his hat.

FITNESS FLASH: Touch your toes 10 times.

* See page ii.

PLACE STICKER HERE

Write the correct time for each clock that has hands. Draw hands on each clock that has a time below it.

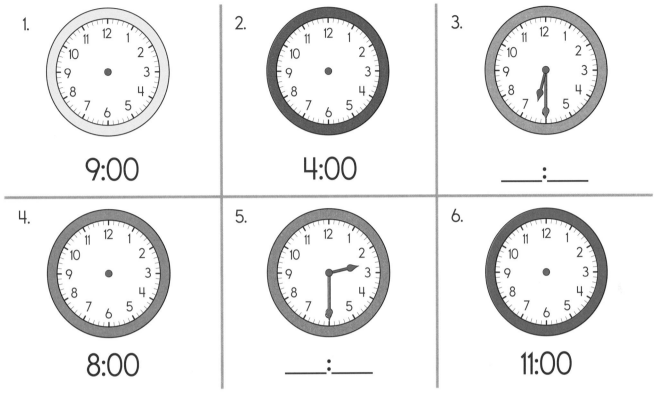

1. 9:00

2. 4:00

3. ___:___

4. 8:00

5. ___:___

6. 11:00

Say the name of each picture. Write the letter of each long vowel sound.

7. ___

8. ___

9. ___

10. ___

11. ___

12. ___

DAY 3

Add endings to write new words for each base word. (Hint: You may need to add an extra letter before the ending in some words.)

Base Word	Add -ed	Add -ing
jump	_____	_____
pat	_____	_____
open	_____	_____
start	_____	_____
touch	_____	_____
blink	_____	_____

Circle the word that names each picture.

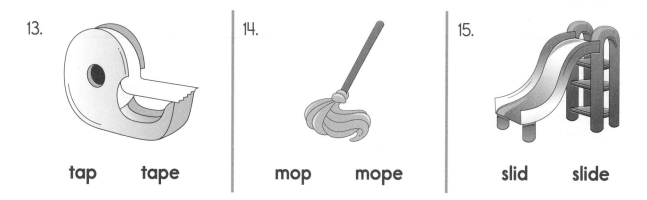

13.

tap   tape

14.

mop   mope

15.

slid   slide

FACTOID: Glass takes one million years to decompose. It can be recycled over and over without wearing out!

PLACE STICKER HERE

Follow the directions to color each shape.

1.

2.

3.

Color one half of the rectangle.

Color one quarter of the circle.

Color two fourths of the rectangle.

Circle the word that names each picture.

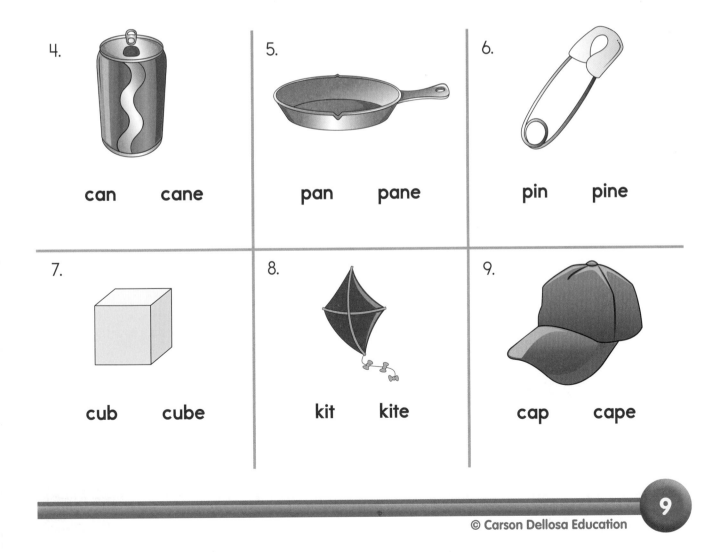

4.

can   cane

5.

pan   pane

6.

pin   pine

7.

cub   cube

8.

kit   kite

9.

cap   cape

DAY 4

Follow the directions to solve each problem.

10. Start with 80. Write the number that is 60 less. _____

11. Start with 90. Write the number that is 40 less. _____

12. Start with 20. Write the number that is 10 less. _____

13. Start with 70. Write the number that is 50 less. _____

14. Start with 60. Write the number that is 30 less. _____

15. Start with 50. Write the number that is 10 less. _____

Write the correct punctuation mark at the end of each sentence.
Use (.), (!), or (?).

16. Do you like carrots_____

17. Are bears fuzzy_____

18. Jan can blow bubbles_____

19. Babies drink milk_____

20. Can you jump rope_____

21. Are clouds white_____

22. That movie was great_____

23. Watch out for that puddle____

24. The woman is happy_____

25. What is your name_____

FITNESS FLASH: Do arm circles for 30 seconds.

* See page ii.

PLACE STICKER HERE

Use each fact family to write two addition and two subtraction number sentences.

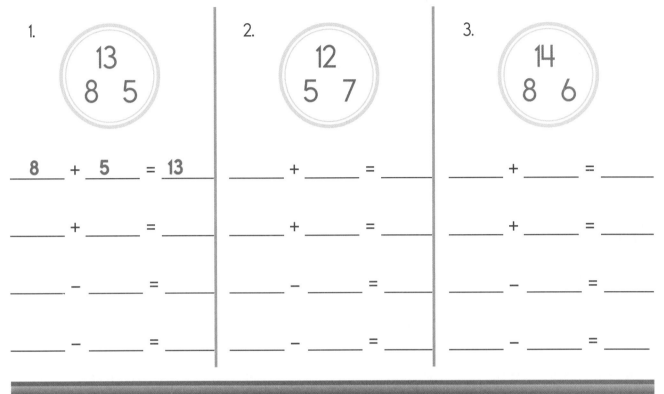

1.

13
8   5

___8___ + ___5___ = __13__

_____ + _____ = _____

_____ − _____ = _____

_____ − _____ = _____

2.

12
5   7

_____ + _____ = _____

_____ + _____ = _____

_____ − _____ = _____

_____ − _____ = _____

3.

14
8   6

_____ + _____ = _____

_____ + _____ = _____

_____ − _____ = _____

_____ − _____ = _____

Say the name of each picture. Write the letter of each short vowel sound.

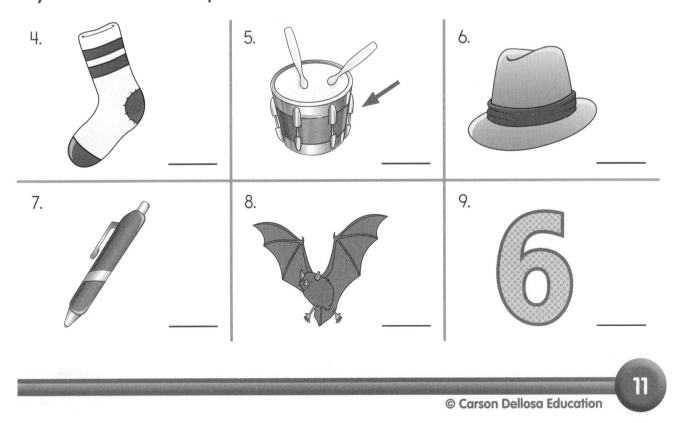

4. ___

5. ___

6. ___

7. ___

8. ___

9. ___

DAY 5

Write each missing addend.

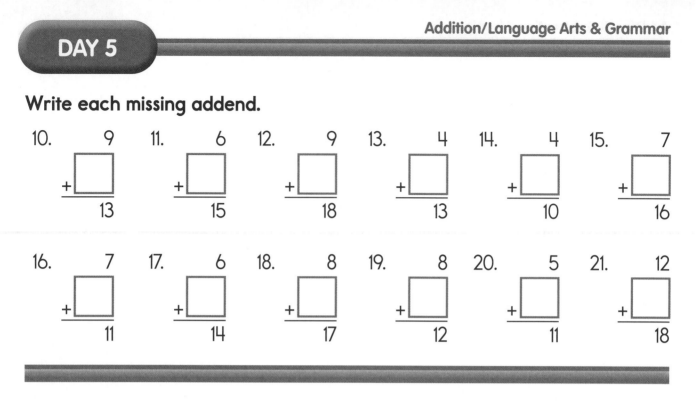

10.   9
    + ☐
      13

11.   6
    + ☐
      15

12.   9
    + ☐
      18

13.   4
    + ☐
      13

14.   4
    + ☐
      10

15.   7
    + ☐
      16

16.   7
    + ☐
      11

17.   6
    + ☐
      14

18.   8
    + ☐
      17

19.   8
    + ☐
      12

20.   5
    + ☐
      11

21.   12
    + ☐
      18

When you write a date, put a comma between the day and the year.

EXAMPLE: January 24, 1936

Add missing commas to the dates below. Use this symbol to add them: ⌄.

22.   My grandma was born on August 5 1948.

23.   Ali had his third birthday on April 18 2013.

24.   On August 11 2001, Mom and Dad got married.

25.   Did you know that the house was finished on June 4 2012?

26.   If Selena was born on October 23 2007, how old is she now?

27.   July 4 1776 is an important day in America's past.

CHARACTER CHECK: Think of a family member who needs your help today. Help her accomplish a task, and you will both feel great.

PLACE STICKER HERE

Count the tens and ones. Write each number.

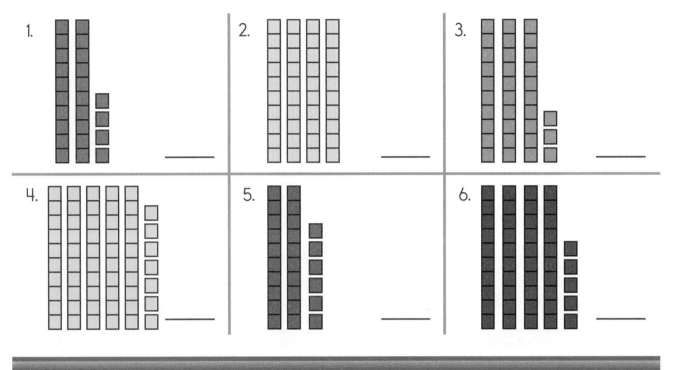

1. _____

2. _____

3. _____

4. _____

5. _____

6. _____

Say the name of each picture. Write the letter of each long vowel sound.

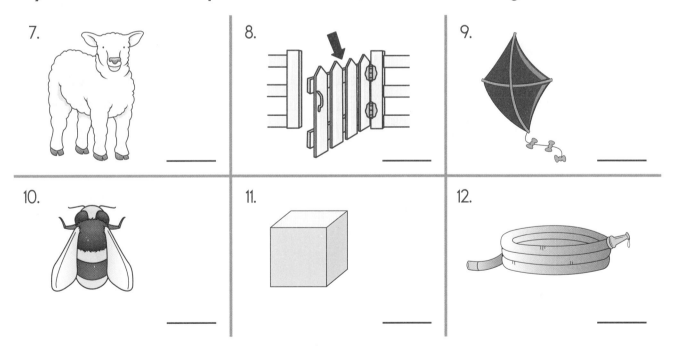

7. _____

8. _____

9. _____

10. _____

11. _____

12. _____

DAY 6

A *root word* is a word that has no endings added to it. On the line, write the root word for each word below.

13. reading _____

14. angrier _____

15. kicking _____

16. watched _____

17. smoother _____

18. happily _____

Move Like a Starfish

Moving around makes you more flexible. Many ocean animals such as crabs, octopuses, and starfish move in unique ways. Practice their ways of getting around. Think about a starfish. It moves by using suction on the bottom of each arm. Pretend that you are a starfish by laying on your stomach, spreading your hands and feet on the floor, and looking facedown. Push up on your toes and hands. Pretend that each of your hands and feet is a starfish foot. Move one "foot" at a time and try to move forward. It requires flexibility to keep your body stretched out. Depending on how far you move like a starfish, you can build strength and endurance, too.

FACTOID: Crocodiles are always growing new teeth to replace teeth they lose.

* See page ii.

PLACE STICKER HERE

Solve each problem.

1. Grayson's train has 8 green cars and 7 red cars. How many train cars does Grayson's train have in all?

2. Twelve deer are standing in a field. Four deer run away. How many deer are left in the field?

3. David has 20 spelling words. He misspells 2 words. How many words does he spell correctly?

4. Magdalena has 13 markers. She finds 6 more markers under her bed. How many markers does Magdalena have in all?

Write how many tens and ones.

5. 46 = _____ tens _____ ones

6. 19 = _____ ten _____ ones

7. 84 = _____ tens _____ ones

8. 64 = _____ tens _____ ones

Write the number.

9. 4 tens and 0 ones = _____

10. 1 ten and 1 one = _____

11. 9 tens and 3 ones = _____

12. 2 tens and 8 ones = _____

DAY 7

Solve the word problems. Write your answer on the line.

13. Hattie picked 8 tulips, 6 daffodils, and 3 violets. How many flowers did she pick in all? _____

14. Henry has 2 sheep, 7 goats, and 9 chickens. How many animals does Henry have?

_____

15. Tariq ate 12 grapes, 3 cherries, and 5 strawberries. How many pieces of fruit did he eat in all? _____

16. Anya spotted 4 frogs, 4 dragonflies, and 6 turtles at the pond. How many animals did she see in all? _____

Circle the word that names each picture.

17.

boy
bone
bow

18.

eagle
egg
eye

19.

sun
sand
snake

FITNESS FLASH: Do 10 shoulder shrugs.

* See page ii.

PLACE STICKER HERE

Circle the number sentences that are true.

1. 7 = 7   2. 8 – 5 = 3

3. 7 = 8   4. 9 – 7 = 3

5. 4 + 3 = 7   6. 6 = 4 + 3

7. 2 + 3 = 5   8. 2 = 1 + 1

9. 7 + 4 = 3   10. 9 = 3 + 6

11. 5 + 2 = 2 + 5   12. 4 + 3 = 3 + 4

13. 4 + 6 = 5 + 3   14. 5 + 6 = 10

Think of three ways to finish this sentence. Write your sentences on the lines.

I liked first grade because . . .

15. _____

_____ .

16. _____

_____ .

17. _____

_____

DAY 8

Circle the word that completes each sentence. Write the word on the line.

18. At night, the sky is _____ .

    day   **dark**   **down**

19. The _____ came to the party.

    game   sun   girls

20. A rabbit can_____to the fence.

    hop   hat   boy

21. Andy's dog got _____ in the pond.

    wet   when   hop

Fill in each blank. Ask an adult if you need help.

When I was a baby, I learned to talk. I learned to talk when I was _____

months old. My first words were _____, _____, and _____

_____. If babies could talk even more, they would tell us _____

_____ .

FACTOID: A person consumes one-tenth of a calorie every time he licks a stamp.

PLACE STICKER HERE

Read the story. Then, answer the questions.

Xander woke up slowly. He stretched. Something felt odd. Was it too early to get up? Xander checked his clock. It was almost 8:00, the same time he always got up in the summer. Xander padded over to the window.

The air looked thick and heavy. He could not see the far side of the yard. Xander ran to the back door. He slipped on some shoes. Then, he went outside. Everything was quiet. It felt like a thick gray blanket lay over the yard. He had never seen fog like this before.

1. What words in the story tell how things look, feel, and sound?

    _____

    _____

    _____

2. Where does the story take place? Describe the place.

    _____

    _____

    _____

3. Write what happened first, next, and last in the story.

    _____

    _____

    _____

DAY 9

Circle the letter of the phrase that tells what each poem is about.

4.   This is a man who is usually wealthy.

He might live a long time if he keeps himself healthy.

His castle's his home, but there's one special thing.

He can always say, "Dad," when he talks to the king.

   A.   a king   B.   a president

   C.   a doctor   D.   a prince

5.   I've never seen them, but I've heard them scurry.

When I open the cupboard door, they leave in a hurry.

They never say please when they take all of our cheese,

And they don't like our big, gray cat Murray.

   A.   relatives   B.   mice

   C.   friends   D.   cats

Find a small object such as a pen, a paper clip, or a toy car. Use it to measure each object below. On the line, write how many times you used the object to measure how long each thing is.

I used _____ as a unit of measurement.

a pillow = _____

a windowsill = _____

a shoe = _____

a box of cereal = _____

a notebook = _____

Draw a line to the mitten that has the answer to each problem.

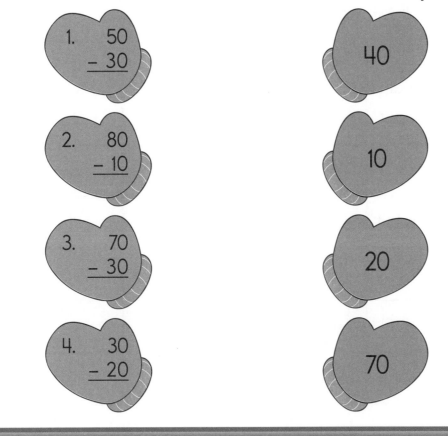

1. $\begin{array}{r} 50 \\ -\ 30 \\ \hline \end{array}$

2. $\begin{array}{r} 80 \\ -\ 10 \\ \hline \end{array}$

3. $\begin{array}{r} 70 \\ -\ 30 \\ \hline \end{array}$

4. $\begin{array}{r} 30 \\ -\ 20 \\ \hline \end{array}$

40

10

20

70

Draw a line to match each sentence with the correct job.

EXAMPLE:

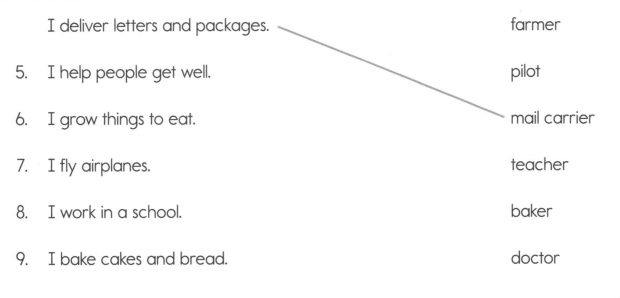

I deliver letters and packages.   farmer

5. I help people get well.   pilot

6. I grow things to eat.   mail carrier

7. I fly airplanes.   teacher

8. I work in a school.   baker

9. I bake cakes and bread.   doctor

DAY 10

Read each word. Color the space blue if the word has the long *i* sound. Color the space green if the word has the short *i* sound.

bib	fry	tie	light	my	sigh	try	wig
six	bike	sign	pie	guy	by	high	if
fib	gift	pit	dry	bite	miss	fish	lit
chin	sit	hill	time	night	hid	bill	quit
bin	mitt	tin	cry	dime	win	fit	will
pin	fine	lie	sight	why	right	shy	fin
zip	ride	buy	side	hike	kite	nine	did

Underline the misspelled word in each sentence. Spell the word correctly on the line.

10. Ebony backed a cake. _____

11. Libby and I whent to the zoo. _____

12. William has a trane. _____

13. Clean your rom! _____

CHARACTER CHECK: Make a list of things you can do to calm down. Then, next time you are upset, refer to your list for help.

PLACE STICKER HERE

Complete each fact family.

1. Family: 2, 3, 5

$2 + 3 = \boxed{}$

$3 + \boxed{} = 5$

$5 - 2 = \boxed{}$

$\boxed{} - 3 = 2$

2. Family: 2, 7, 9

$7 + 2 = \boxed{}$

$\boxed{} + 7 = 9$

$9 - \boxed{} = 2$

$9 - \boxed{} = 7$

3. Family: 3, 5, 8

$5 + 3 = \boxed{}$

$\boxed{} + \boxed{} = 8$

$8 - \boxed{} = \boxed{}$

$\boxed{} - 3 = \boxed{}$

Changing the order of addends in an addition sentence does not change the answer. Complete the sentences below.

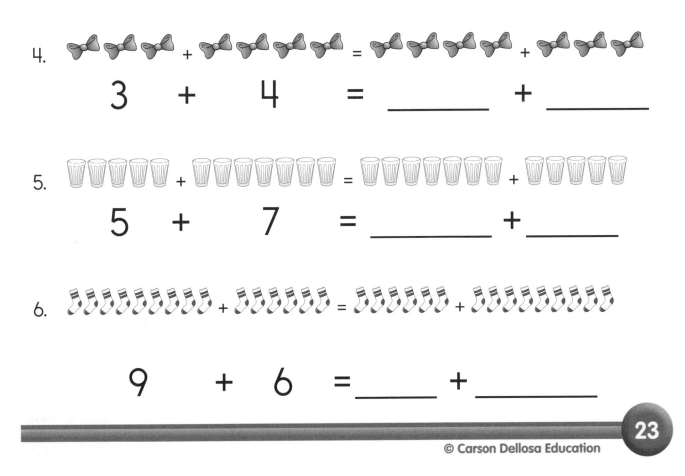

4. $3 \quad + \quad 4 \quad = \underline{} + \underline{}$

5. $5 \quad + \quad 7 \quad = \underline{} + \underline{}$

6. $9 \quad + \quad 6 \quad = \underline{} + \underline{}$

DAY 11

Read the story. Answer the questions.

At the Pond

One warm, spring day, some ducklings decided to go to a pond. They wanted to go swim.

"Can we go too?" asked the chicks.

"Chicks can't swim," laughed the ducklings.

"We will run in the tall grass and look for bugs. Please let us go with you," begged the chicks. So, the ducklings and the chicks set off for the pond.

The ducklings swam in the pond. They splashed in the water. The chicks ran in the tall grass. They looked for bugs. The ducklings and the chicks had fun.

After a while, the ducklings and the chicks were tired from playing. They missed their mothers. They missed their nests. It was time to go home.

7. Which sentence tells the main idea of the story?

    A. Ducklings have fun swimming.

    B. Chicks and ducklings hatch from eggs.

    C. The ducklings and the chicks had fun at the pond.

8. Number the story events in order.

    _____The ducklings swam while the chicks ran in the grass.

    _____The ducklings wanted to go to the pond.

    _____The ducklings and the chicks were tired. It was time to go home.

FACTOID: Donkeys can see all four of their feet at the same time.

PLACE STICKER HERE

You can group addends in addition sentences in different ways without changing the sum. Write the missing numbers on the lines.

1. $4 + 8 + 2 = 4 + 10 = $ _____

2. $10 + $ _____ $ = 5 + 5 + 9 = 19$

3. $6 + 6 + 4 = $ _____ $ + 6 = 16$

4. $3 + 7 + $ _____ $ = 10 + 1 = 11$

5. $9 + 1 + 8 = 10 + 8 = $ _____

6. $10 + 0 + 2 = 10 + $ _____ $ = 12$

In a blend, like *sl* in *slide*, two consonants make a sound together. Say the name of each picture. Write the letters for the blend in each word.

7.

_____ _____

8.

_____ _____

9.

_____ _____

10.

_____ _____

11.

_____ _____

12.

_____ _____

DAY 12

Look at each number in the apple. On the apple to the left, write the number that is 10 less than the number shown. On the apple to the right, write the number that is 10 more.

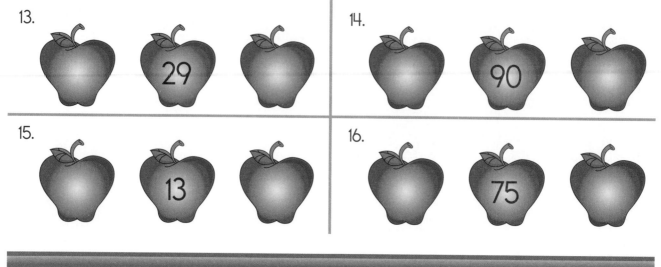

13.   29

14.   90

15.   13

16.   75

Unscramble each sentence. Write the words in the correct order.

17.   swim like Ducks to.

_____

18.   we sandbox Can play in the?

_____

19.   nests birds in trees Some make.

_____

20.   fun today Are having you?

_____

FITNESS FLASH: Do 10 shoulder shrugs.

* See page ii.

PLACE STICKER HERE

Each sentence is missing at least one capital letter. Make three small lines under letters that should be capitals (<u>f</u>).

1. Myles kicked the ball to stella.

2. Coach rodrigo asked me to go first.

3. kerry scored four home runs in august!

4. Antonio's soccer game is on july 8th.

Say the name of each picture. Circle the pictures that have the long *a* sound, as in *tape*.

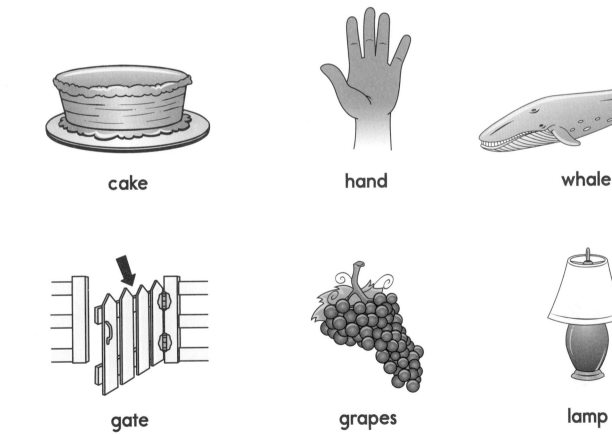

cake   hand   whale

gate   grapes   lamp

DAY 13

Rewrite each set of words below to make it show ownership.

EXAMPLE: the pear belonging to Peter
Peter's pear

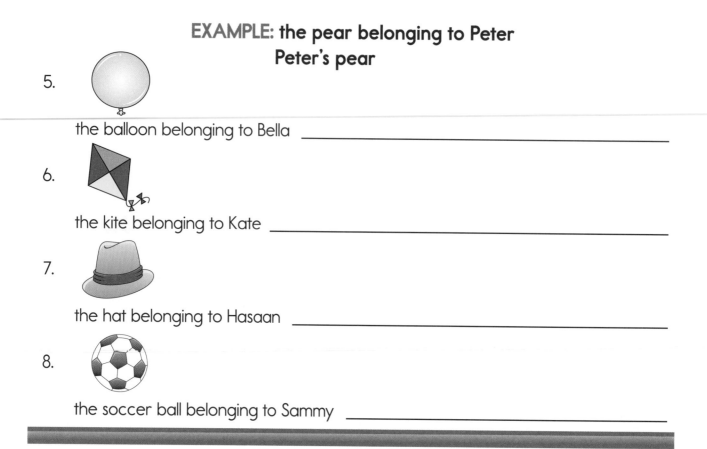

5. the balloon belonging to Bella _____

6. the kite belonging to Kate _____

7. the hat belonging to Hasaan _____

8. the soccer ball belonging to Sammy _____

Read the word on each balloon. Color the balloon red if the word has the long *u* sound. Color the balloon blue if the word has the short *u* sound.

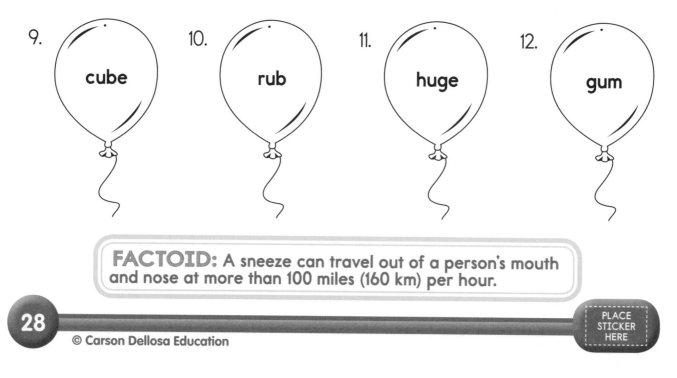

9. cube

10. rub

11. huge

12. gum

FACTOID: A sneeze can travel out of a person's mouth and nose at more than 100 miles (160 km) per hour.

PLACE STICKER HERE

Complete each fact family.

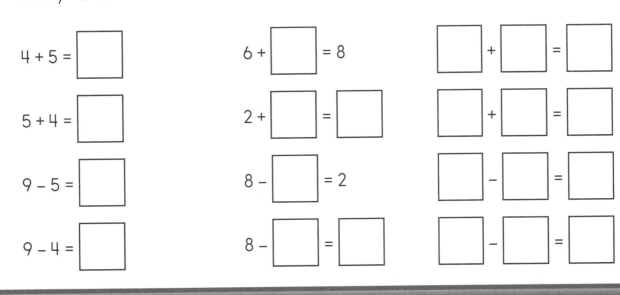

1. Family: 4, 9, 5

    4 + 5 = ☐

    5 + 4 = ☐

    9 – 5 = ☐

    9 – 4 = ☐

2. Family: 6, 2, 8

    6 + ☐ = 8

    2 + ☐ = ☐

    8 – ☐ = 2

    8 – ☐ = ☐

3. Family: 3, 7, 10

    ☐ + ☐ = ☐

    ☐ + ☐ = ☐

    ☐ – ☐ = ☐

    ☐ – ☐ = ☐

Read each noun in the box. Write it in the correct column.

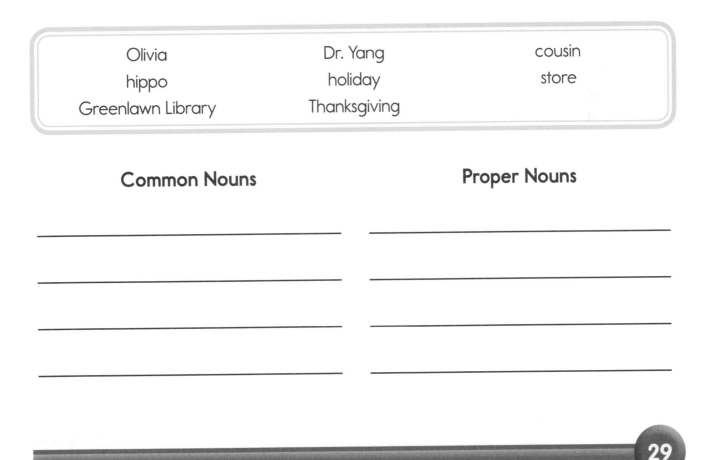

Olivia	Dr. Yang	cousin
hippo	holiday	store
Greenlawn Library	Thanksgiving	

Common Nouns

_____

_____

_____

_____

Proper Nouns

_____

_____

_____

_____

DAY 14

Circle the letter of the sentence that describes each picture.

4.   A.   Dez walked up the stairs.

     B.   Dez walked down the stairs.

     C.   Dez sat on the stairs.

5.   A.   Justin threw the baseball to his dad.

     B.   Justin threw the baseball to Jessica.

     C.   Justin threw the baseball to his mom.

Some pronouns tell who owns something. Write a word from the box to replace each word in bold type.

her	my	his	their

6.   **Harry's** birthday = _____ birthday

7.   **Vijay's** and **Vic's** puppies = _____ puppies

8.   **Hanna's** life jacket = _____ life jacket

9.   the sweater **belonging to me** = _____ sweater

FITNESS FLASH: Do arm circles for 30 seconds.

* See page ii.

PLACE STICKER HERE

Solve each problem.

1. Iman has 9 baseballs. He finds 3 more. How many baseballs does he have in all?

2. A farmer has 12 apples. He makes a pie with 5 of them. How many apples does he have left?

Respect Reminder

What does it mean to respect someone? It means to think about someone else's feelings and to show the person that you care. List the names of the three people whom you respect most and tell why. Then, write how you can show them respect. At the top of your list, write *Respect Really Rules!*

_____

_____

_____

_____

_____

_____

Read the story. Answer the questions.

A Place for Little Frog

Little Frog hopped out of the pond. "Where are you going, Little Frog?" asked the other frogs.

"I am tired of living in this pond with so many frogs," he said. "I need more space." So, Little Frog hopped away.

Soon, he met a bee. When he told the bee his story, the bee buzzed, "You cannot live with me. You would get stuck in my honey."

Little Frog said, "Don't worry, bee, your hive is not the place for me."

Next, Little Frog met a dog. The dog barked and chased Little Frog away. "Living with a dog is not the place for me," said Little Frog.

Little Frog hopped and hopped all of the way back to his pond. The other frogs were happy to see him. They moved over to make room for him. Little Frog settled in, smiled, and said, "Now, this is the place for me."

3. Which sentence tells the main idea of the story?

    A. A hive is no place for a frog.

    B. Dogs do not like frogs.

    C. Little Frog found out that his own home is best.

4. Number the story events in order.

    _____ Little Frog hopped all of the way back to his pond.

    _____ Little Frog hopped out of the pond.

    _____ A dog chased Little Frog away.

CHARACTER CHECK: Share with a friend a time when he showed you kindness.

PLACE STICKER HERE

Write a letter to tell what kind of sentence each one is.

S = Statement   Q = Question   C = Command   E = Exclamation

1. _____ What time does the game start?

2. _____ Zane just hit a home run!

3. _____ Pass me the bug spray.

4. _____ Oliver is on first base.

5. _____ Destiny is the fastest runner on our team.

Choose the conjunction that completes each sentence. Write it on the line.

6. Drew _____ Mom went to the farmers' market.
   (and, but)

7. Do you like corn _____ carrots better?
   (or, but)

8. The market had eggs, _____ we will have omelets today.
   (or, so)

9. Drew loves peas, _____ all the farmers were sold out.
   (but, because)

Fill in the circle beside the sentence that best describes each picture.

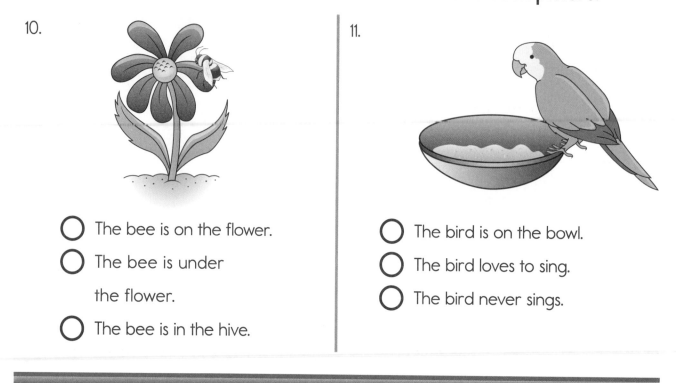

10.

○ The bee is on the flower.

○ The bee is under
the flower.

○ The bee is in the hive.

11.

○ The bird is on the bowl.

○ The bird loves to sing.

○ The bird never sings.

Say the name of each picture. Write **1** if the word has one syllable.
Write **2** if the word has two syllables.

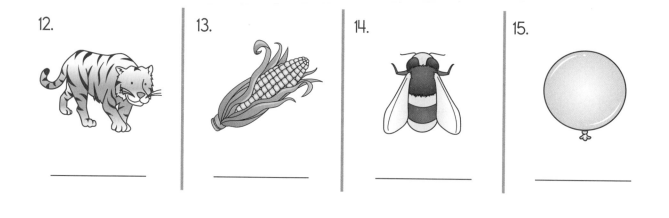

12.

_____

13.

_____

14.

_____

15.

_____

FACTOID: Although a polar bear appears to be white, its
skin is black. Its fur is actually many colorless, hollow tubes.

PLACE
STICKER
HERE

Add the word parts. Write the new word on the line.

1. melt + ed = _____

2. sweet + er = _____

3. un + tie = _____

4. fear + ful = _____

5. re + read = _____

6. pre + heat = _____

Say the name of each picture. Write the letter of each vowel sound.

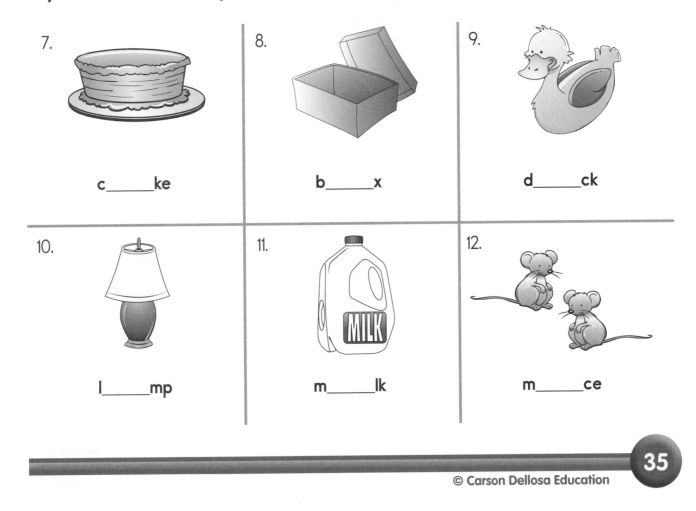

7. c_____ke

8. b_____x

9. d_____ck

10. l_____mp

11. m_____lk

12. m_____ce

DAY 17

Write the word or phrase that tells where each shape is. The shapes are *on top of*, *under*, or *next to* other shapes.

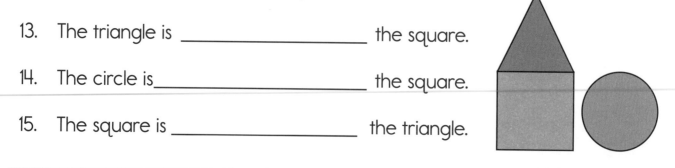

13. The triangle is _____ the square.

14. The circle is_____ the square.

15. The square is _____ the triangle.

Draw a line to match each butterfly to the flower with the same long vowel sound.

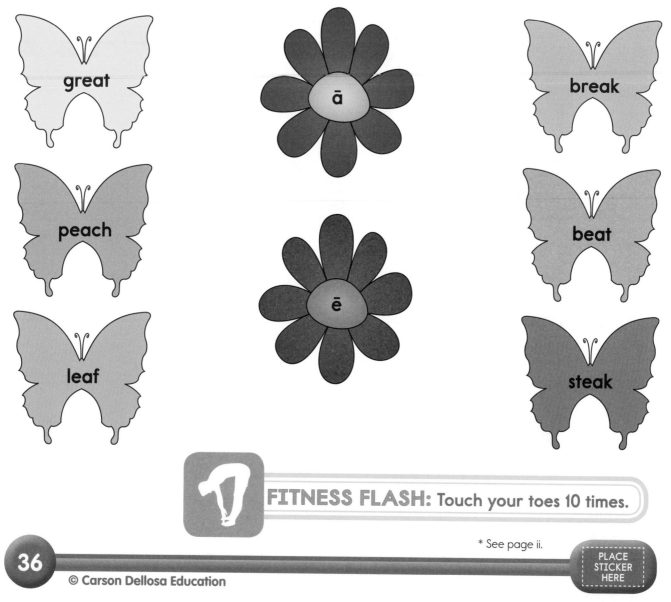

great

break

peach

beat

leaf

steak

ā

ē

FITNESS FLASH: Touch your toes 10 times.

* See page ii.

PLACE STICKER HERE

Write how many tens and ones are in each number.
EXAMPLE:

26 = __2__ tens __6__ ones   1.   41 = _____ tens _____ one

2.   45 = _____ tens _____ ones   3.   84 = _____ tens _____ ones

4.   65 = _____ tens _____ ones   5.   72 = _____ tens _____ ones

6.   17 = _____ tens _____ ones   7.   39 = _____ tens _____ ones

8.   50 = _____ tens _____ ones   9.   51 = _____ tens _____ one

10.   97 = _____ tens _____ ones   11.   100 = _____ tens _____ ones

Write a paragraph for a younger brother or sister, cousin, or friend. Explain how to do something step by step. You could explain how to feed a pet, make a sandwich, or plant a seed.

_____

_____

_____

_____

_____

_____

_____

DAY 18

Number the sentences in the order that the events happened.

12. _____ The sun came out. It became a pretty day.

13. _____ It started to rain.

14. _____ Hannah put her umbrella away.

15. _____ Hannah used her umbrella.

16. _____ The clouds came, and the sky was dark.

What do you think the perfect tree house would look like? Describe it and draw a picture of it.

_____

_____

_____

_____

_____

_____

_____

FACTOID: Dust from Africa can travel all the way to Florida.

PLACE STICKER HERE

Write > or < to compare each set of numbers.

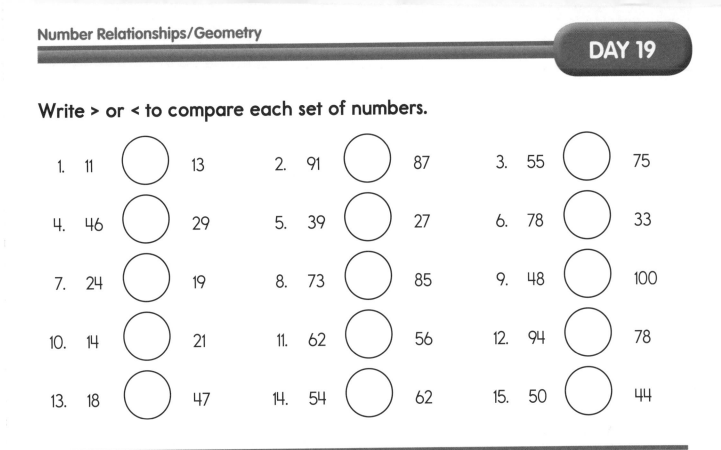

1. 11 ◯ 13

2. 91 ◯ 87

3. 55 ◯ 75

4. 46 ◯ 29

5. 39 ◯ 27

6. 78 ◯ 33

7. 24 ◯ 19

8. 73 ◯ 85

9. 48 ◯ 100

10. 14 ◯ 21

11. 62 ◯ 56

12. 94 ◯ 78

13. 18 ◯ 47

14. 54 ◯ 62

15. 50 ◯ 44

Use the directions to draw shapes.

16. Draw a shape that has no sides and no corners.

17. Draw a shape that has three sides and three corners.

18. Draw a shape that has four sides of equal length.

19. Draw a shape with four sides and four corners. Opposite sides are equal in length.

Solve each riddle.

20. I am tiny. I have three body parts and six legs. I can be a real pest at picnics. I

    am an _____.

21. I was just born. My mom and dad feed me. I cry and sleep, but I cannot walk. I

    am a _____.

22. I am made of metal and can be small. I can lock doors and unlock them, too. I

    am a _____.

23. I have four legs. I like to play. I bark. I am a _____.

Mount Flex

Become flexible by pretending that you are rock climbing. Lie on your back and stretch your right arm out in front of you as far as you can. Now, stretch your left leg out in front of you toward the sky. Stretch it as far as it will go. Switch arms and legs. Repeat 10 times. Move slowly as you climb the "mountain."

FITNESS FLASH: Practice a V-sit. Stretch five times.

* See page ii.

PLACE STICKER HERE

Write the correct time for each clock that has hands. Draw hands on each clock that has a time below it.

1. 2:30

2. ___:___

3. 10:30

4. ___:___

5. 5:00

6. ___:___

Say the name of each picture. Circle the letters that make each beginning sound.

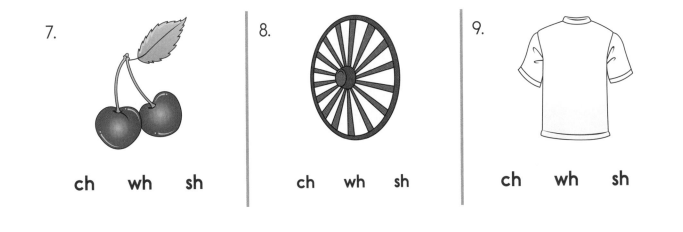

7. ch   wh   sh

8. ch   wh   sh

9. ch   wh   sh

DAY 20

Write *1, 2,* or *3* on each line to order the objects from shortest to longest.

10. 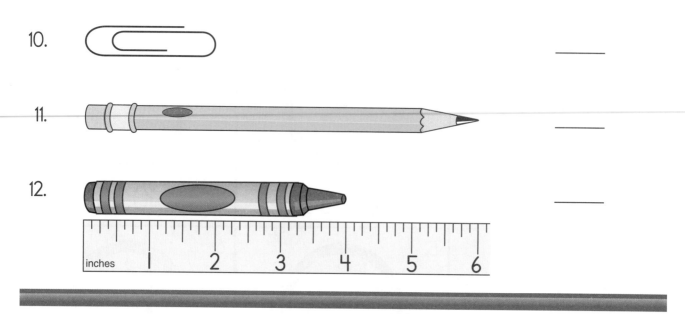 _____

11. _____

12. _____

A title tells what a story is about. Write the letter of the title next to the story it matches.

TITLES

A. The Turtle Dream   B. The Sleepover   C. A Wish Before Bed

13. _____ Jenna made a wish every night before going to sleep. She would look in the sky for the brightest star. Then, she would close her eyes and make a wish.

14. _____ Malia fell asleep in the car on the way to the beach. She dreamed that she was a flying turtle. She flew all around the beach. No one could catch her.

15. _____ Kendra had her friend Leslie sleep over. They watched a movie and ate popcorn. They made a tent out of blankets. They slept in the tent.

CHARACTER CHECK: Discuss with an adult what you think is the most important of all good manners.

PLACE STICKER HERE

Upside-Down Water

Can you turn a cup of water upside down without spilling it?

Materials:
- index card
- clear plastic cup
- water

Procedure:
1. Do this experiment over a sink.
2. Fill the cup halfway with water.
3. Put the index card on top of the cup. Put your hand over the card. Turn the cup upside down over the sink.
4. Wait two seconds. Then, move your hand away.

What's This All About?
When you flip the cup, the air outside of the cup pushes on the card. The air pushes harder than the water inside the cup. If you wiggle the card before you move your hand, the water molecules on the card and the rim of the cup will stick together. Then, air cannot get in and equalize the pressure.

More Fun Ideas to Try:
- Use different amounts of water in the cup.
- Try different types of paper. You can use construction paper, wrapping paper or notebook paper.
- Find out how long you can hold the cup upside down before water starts to spill out.
- Try plastic cups of different sizes and shapes.
- Write a letter or an e-mail to a friend or relative. Tell about the experiment you did. Explain how it works and what your results were.

BONUS

The Flying Sheet of Paper

How do planes fly?

Materials:

- sheet of paper

Procedure:

1. Hold a sheet of paper just under your bottom lip. Curve the top of the paper slightly. What do you think will happen to the paper if you blow down and across the top of it? Do you think it will hit you in the chest, stay where it is, or bounce up and hit you in the nose?
2. Write your prediction on a separate sheet of paper.
3. Blow down and across the top of the paper.

What's This All About?

By blowing down and across the top of the paper, you cause air molecules to move faster across the paper rather than moving around as they normally do. Faster moving air molecules lower the air pressure on the top of the paper. Higher air pressure under the paper pushes the paper up. For an airplane to fly, the air pressure must be lower on top of the wings than under them. The higher air pressure under the wings pushes the airplane up.

More Fun Ideas to Try:

The next time you take a shower, notice what the shower curtain does. Does it balloon away, or does it move closer to you? Do you know why?

My Own Map

Maps have many uses. A pilot uses maps to find the right flight paths. A hiker uses a map to find her way on a trail. A traveler uses a map to get around a new town.

Work on your mapmaking skills by drawing a map of a path that is in or around your home. You will need a sheet of paper and a pencil. Be as accurate as possible. If you are drawing a path from your room to the refrigerator, include hallways, stairways, rooms, and furniture that you pass as you walk.

Try your map when it is finished. Follow the path as you drew it. Make changes if needed. Then, have a friend or family member try your map. Ask her to use the map to follow the path to the end. Have a surprise treat waiting for her, such as a snack to share.

BONUS

The State of Things

It is important to learn about where you live. Your state or province might be the home of the first candy factory or the only state or province with a professional trampoline team. With an adult, search the Internet to find interesting information about where you live. Share the fun facts with family and friends. Below are some search terms to get you started:

• facts about [your state or province name]

• government site for kids

• local library website

International Cuisine

You can learn a lot about other countries by making and eating some of their native dishes. Think of a country you would like to know more about. Find out what foods the people from that country eat. For example, if you want to learn about France, go to the library with an adult and check out French cookbooks or books about French food. Or, search the Internet with an adult to find recipes for French dishes.

Choose a simple recipe with ingredients that you and an adult can buy at your local grocery store. Whether you make soup, salad, or another treat from the country, you will "taste" a bit of the country when you eat the food. Get your family involved. Invite each family member to choose a country and enjoy trying different foods from places around the world.

* See page ii.

BONUS

Take It Outside!

In many places, the weather is beautiful outside during the summer. The sun shines. Bright flowers bloom. Color is everywhere. Nature is as pretty as a picture. Make your own art from things that you find outside during the summer. Collect the objects that you discover, such as leaves, stones, shells, flowers, bark, and sticks. Then, make a colorful collage from your treasures.

Grow a plant! All you need is a hand shovel, a seed or seedling, some soil, sunshine, and water. Ask an adult to help you choose what to plant and where to plant it. Whether you plant in a pot or in the ground, it's amazing to give new life to something special. After you plant the seed or seedling, put a paint stirrer or a wooden craft stick in the ground beside it. Then, use a pen to mark the plant's height as it grows taller. Spend the summer watering your plant and watching it grow!

Head outside with a sheet of paper and pencil. Look around and list the things that you see, such as a bush, an ant, a cat, a sidewalk, a bee, a mailbox, a car, and a street. Sort the words into categories. Try to think of at least three ways to sort your words. For example, you could sort the words by their beginning sounds or by whether they name living or nonliving things.

* See page ii.

Monthly Goals

Think of three goals to set for yourself this month. For example, you may want to spend more time reading with your family. Have an adult help you write your goals on the lines.

Place a sticker next to each of your goals that you complete. Feel proud that you have met your goals!

1. _____

2. _____

3. _____

Word List

The following words are used in this section. They are good words for you to know. Read each word aloud with an adult. When you see a word from this list on a page, circle it with your favorite color of crayon.

adjective	passage
attempts	strength
describe	struggle
difference	tally
habitat	vanish

Introduction to Strength

This section includes fitness and character development activities that focus on strength. These activities are designed to get your child moving and to get him thinking about strengthening his body and his character. If your child has limited mobility, feel free to modify any suggested exercises to fit individual abilities.

Physical Strength

Like flexibility, strength is an important component of good health. Many children may think that the only people who are strong are the people who can lift an enormous amount of weight. However, strength is more than the ability to pick up heavy dumbbells. Explain that strength is built over time, and point out to your child how much stronger he has become since he was a toddler.

Everyday activities and many fun exercises provide opportunities for children to gain strength. Your child could carry grocery bags to build his arms, ride a bicycle to develop his legs, or swim for a full-body strength workout. Classic exercises, such as push-ups and chin-ups, are also fantastic strength builders.

Help your child set realistic, achievable goals to improve his strength based on the activities that he enjoys. Over the summer months, offer encouragement and praise as your child gains strength and accomplishes his strength goals.

Strength of Character

As your child is building his physical strength, guide him to work on his inner strength as well. Explain that having strong character means standing up for his values, even if others do not agree with his viewpoint. Explain that it is not always easy to show inner strength. Discuss real-life examples, such as a time that he may have been teased by another child. How did he use his inner strength to handle the situation?

Remind your child that inner strength can be shown in many ways. For example, your child can show strength by being honest, by standing up for someone who needs his help, and by putting his best efforts into every task. Use your time together over the summer to help your child develop his strength, both physically and emotionally. Look for moments to acknowledge when he has demonstrated strength of character so that he can see the positive growth that he has achieved on the inside.

Skip-count by fives. Fill in the missing numbers.

1. 60 ___ 70 75 ___ ___ 90 95

Skip-count by tens. Fill in the missing numbers.

2. 320 ___ 340 350 ___ 370 ___ 390

Skip-count by hundreds. Fill in the missing numbers.

3. 300 400 ___ ___ 700 ___ 900 1,000

Write adjectives to describe each object.

4. teddy bear

_____

_____

_____

_____

5. gift

_____

_____

_____

_____

Unscramble each sentence. Write the words in the correct order.

6. sun shine today will The.

   _____

7. mile today I a walked.

   _____

8. fence We painted our.

   _____

9. me knit will She something for.

   _____

Follow the directions to solve each problem.

10. Start with 54. Write the number that is 100 more. _____

11. Start with 80. Write the number that is 10 more. _____

12. Start with 22. Write the number that is 100 more. _____

13. Start with 65. Write the number that is 10 more. _____

FACTOID: Sloths move so slowly that green algae can grow on their fur.

PLACE STICKER HERE

Circle the greater number in each set.

1. 17 **or** 71

2. 91 **or** 19

3. 67 **or** 72

4. 34 **or** 30

5. 26 **or** 41

6. 29 **or** 40

7. 90 **or** 99

8. 79 **or** 80

9. 44 **or** 54

Circle the word that names each picture. Write the word on the line.

10.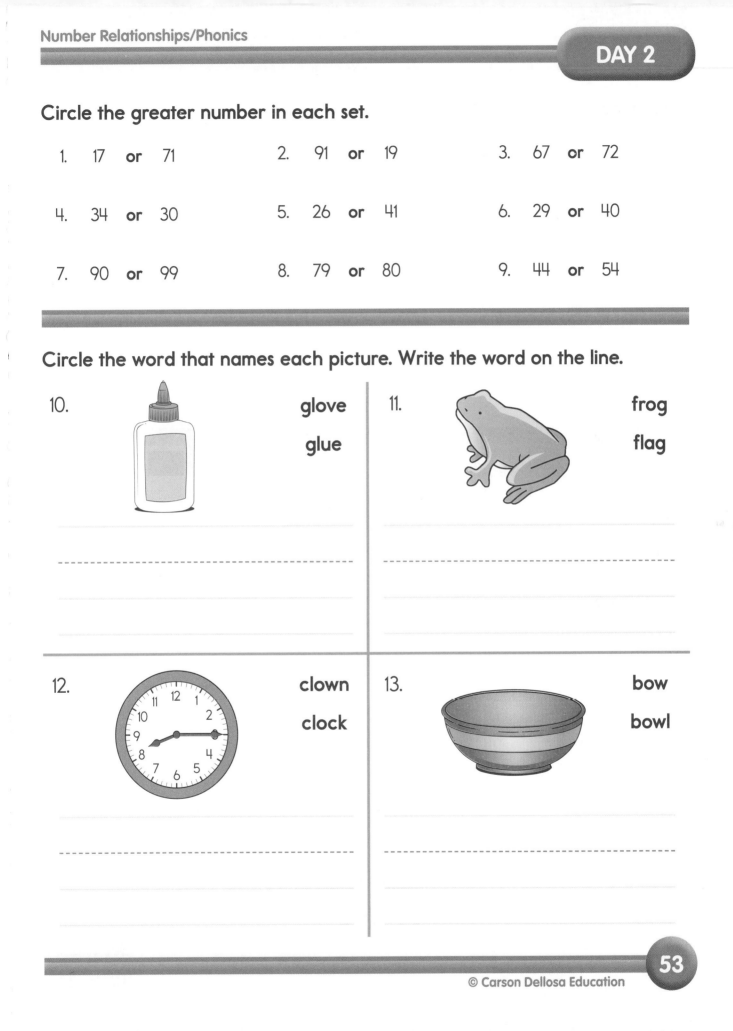
    glove

    glue

11.
    frog

    flag

12.
    clown

    clock

13.
    bow

    bowl

Read each paragraph. Circle the letter of the best title.

14. Carlos is at bat. He hits the ball. He runs to first base and then to second base. Will Carlos make it all of the way to home plate?

   A.   Running

   B.   Carlos Likes to Play

   C.   Carlos's Baseball Game

15. Madison put on sunscreen and sunglasses. Then, she found her favorite green hat. Madison was ready to go outside.

   A.   A Rainy Day

   B.   Ready to Go Out in the Sun

   C.   Madison Likes to Play

Draw a line to match each contraction to its word pair.

EXAMPLE:

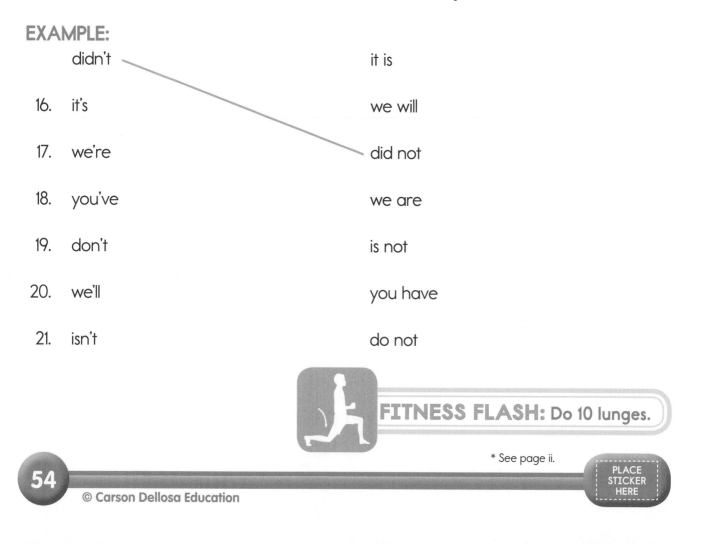

      didn't   it is

16. it's   we will

17. we're   did not

18. you've   we are

19. don't   is not

20. we'll   you have

21. isn't   do not

FITNESS FLASH: Do 10 lunges.

* See page ii.

PLACE STICKER HERE

Solve each problem.

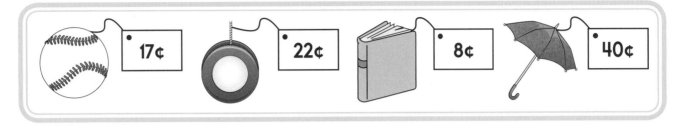

17¢   22¢   8¢   40¢

1. Lori bought an umbrella and a book. How much money did she spend?

2. Henry bought a yo-yo and an umbrella. How much money did he spend?

3. Maria bought a baseball and a yo-yo. How much money did she spend?

4. Alejandro bought a baseball and a book. How much money did he spend?

Leapfrog

Play a fun game of leapfrog to show your strength. Find a friend, sibling, or parent to join you. To play, have one person crouch down low. Have the second person place her hands on the crouching person's back and hop over him. For the first round, pretend that you are frogs. Play more rounds and transform into other hopping creatures, such as grasshoppers, rabbits, and kangaroos. Each time that you hop, remember that you are making your legs stronger and your body healthier! For a bigger strength challenge, invite friends and family members to form a line of crouching critters for you to jump over.

* See page ii.

DAY 3

Add to find each sum.

5.   5   6.   8   7.   3   8.   9   9.   15   10.   10
     +7   +4   +7   +5   + 2   + 6

Subtract to find each difference.

11.   12   12.   9   13.   11   14.   8   15.   10   16.   1 6
    – 8   –4   – 7   –8   – 2   – 2

Write the word that matches each set of clues.
EXAMPLE:

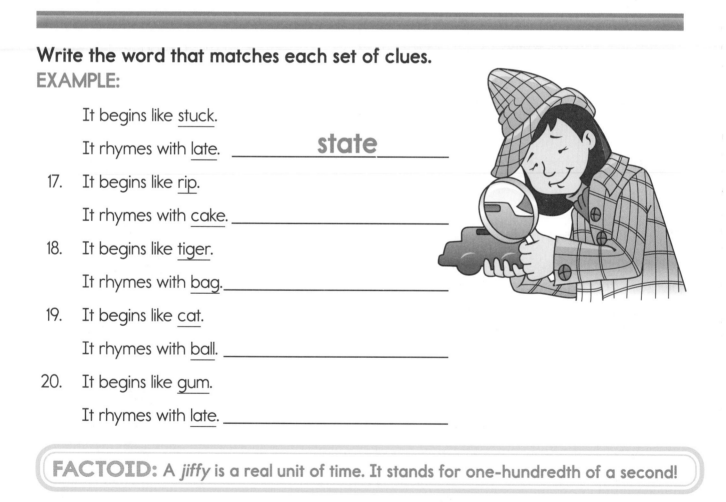

It begins like <u>st</u>uck.

It rhymes with <u>late</u>. _____ state _____

17.   It begins like <u>r</u>ip.

     It rhymes with <u>cake</u>. _____

18.   It begins like <u>t</u>iger.

     It rhymes with <u>bag</u>._____

19.   It begins like <u>c</u>at.

     It rhymes with <u>ball</u>. _____

20.   It begins like <u>g</u>um.

     It rhymes with <u>late</u>. _____

FACTOID: A *jiffy* is a real unit of time. It stands for one-hundredth of a second!

PLACE
STICKER
HERE

Similar words can have different shades of meaning. Underline the word that best completes each sentence.

1. Jamilla carefully (sipped, gulped) the hot tea.

2. Dana (tapped, pounded) on her parents' door when she heard the fire alarm.

3. Lex felt (nervous, terrified) when he realized he had forgotten his permission slip.

4. Dad was (tired, exhausted) after driving all through the night to get home.

How many are in each group? Write the number on the line. Then, circle *odd* or *even*.

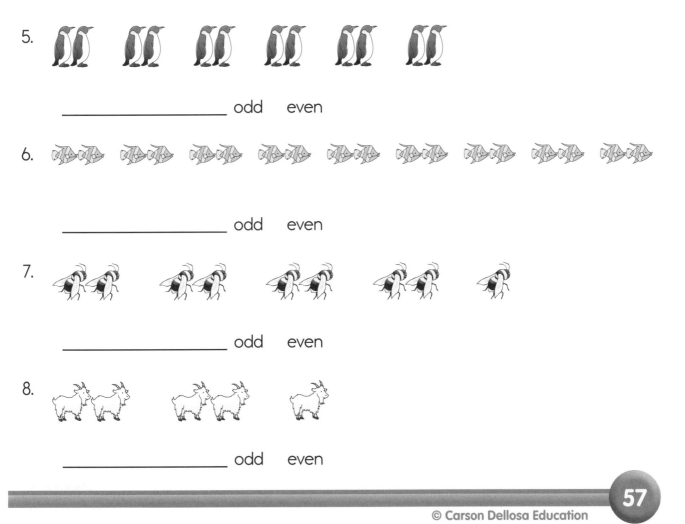

5. _____ odd   even

6. _____ odd   even

7. _____ odd   even

8. _____ odd   even

DAY 4

Say each word in the box. Listen for the long vowel sound. Write the word under the correct heading.

bugle	apron	bedtime	Monday	human
eagle	rider	argue	flavor	hello
frozen	ocean	unkind	season	fever

Long a	Long e	Long i	Long o	Long u
_____	_____	_____	_____	_____
_____	_____	_____	_____	_____
_____	_____	_____	_____	_____

Underline the misspelled word in each sentence. Then, write each misspelled word correctly on the line.

9. What may I help yu with?_____

10. Please giv him a fork. _____

11. You can sti on the chair. _____

12. Will you miks the paint? _____

FITNESS FLASH: Do five push-ups.

* See page ii.

PLACE STICKER HERE

58

Which flavor of ice cream is the most popular with your friends and family? Ask each person to choose a favorite ice-cream flavor from the list. Make a tally mark beside each answer given.

vanilla _____   banana _____

chocolate _____   cherry _____

strawberry _____   other _____

Count the tally marks beside each flavor. Graph your results.

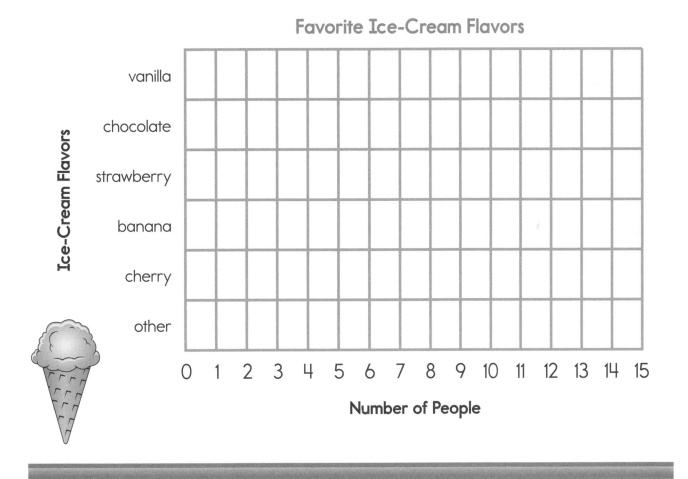

Favorite Ice-Cream Flavors

Ice-Cream Flavors

vanilla
chocolate
strawberry
banana
cherry
other

0 1 2 3 4 5 6 7 8 9 10 11 12 13 14 15

Number of People

Describe the funniest dream you have ever had. Write about it on a separate sheet of paper.

DAY 5

Read the story. Answer the questions.

Olivia lives on a farm. She wakes up early to do chores. Olivia feeds all the horses and chickens. She also collects the eggs. Sometimes, she helps her dad milk the cows. Her favorite thing to do in the morning is eat breakfast.

1. Where does Olivia live? _____

2. Why does she wake up early? _____

3. Write one chore that Olivia does. _____

4. What is her favorite thing to do in the morning? _____

_____

Say the name of each picture. Write the vowels to complete each word.

5.

c_____ _____n

6.

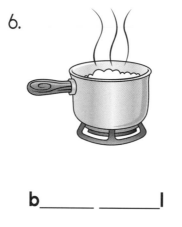

b_____ _____l

7.

_____ _____l

CHARACTER CHECK: Form a neighborhood cleanup crew. With an adult and some friends, walk through your neighborhood and pick up litter. Your neighborhood will be a cleaner place!

PLACE STICKER HERE

Add to find each sum.

1. 2
    2
    +2

2. 1
    1
    +1

3. 4
    4
    +4

4. 5
    5
    +5

5. 2
    3
    +2

6. 4
    3
    +0

7. 5
    4
    +5

8. 3
    3
    +3

9. 4
    6
    +5

10. 6
    4
    +2

11. 7
    0
    +7

12. 10
    10
    +10

Rain Forest Animals

Have you ever seen the way animals of the rain forests move? Some animals, such as monkeys, swing from tree branch to tree branch. Some animals, such as sloths, slowly climb trees by stretching up and down. Read about a rain forest animal. Then, create your own stretch. Try to move like your chosen animal. Share your new stretch with a friend. Can she guess which animal you are?

* See page ii.

DAY 6

Draw a line to match each pair that has the same difference.

13. 5 – 3   5 – 1

     8 – 3   9 – 8

     8 – 4   7 – 2

     5 – 4   6 – 4

14. 8 – 7   10 – 4

     3 – 1   4 – 3

     8 – 2   5 – 3

     9 – 5   7 – 3

15. 10 – 5   13 –10

     12 – 6   7 – 1

     2 – 0   9 – 4

     9 – 6   4 – 2

16. 5 – 5   14 – 7

     12 – 9   8 – 5

     11 – 4   8 – 8

     12 – 8   5 – 1

Unscramble each word. Spell each word correctly on the line to complete each sentence.

17. Juan had a _____ for _____ mother.
                   igft   **ihs**

18. The _____ has a _____ tire.
            acr   **tfla**

19. A butterfly _____ on _____ flower.
                   ats   **hte**

20. My _____ works at the _____.
          add   **tsoer**

FACTOID: You'll never see elephants playing hopscotch. Why? Because they can't jump!

PLACE STICKER HERE

Read each paragraph. Underline the sentence that states the main idea.

1. Sidney's umbrella is old. It has holes in it. The color is faded. It doesn't keep the rain off of her.

2. Tabby is a farm cat. He is tan and white. Tabby helps the farmer by catching mice in the barn. He sleeps on soft hay.

3. Big, gray clouds are in the sky. The wind is blowing, and it is getting colder. I think it will snow.

Solve the word problems.

4. Amina has three shelves. One is 14 inches tall, one is 18 inches tall, and one is 21 inches tall. If she stacks all three of them, how tall will her shelves be?

    _____

5. On Friday, the high temperature was 86°. It dropped 20° by midnight. What was the temperature at midnight?

    _____

6. The first time Dylan measured his sunflower, it was 34 inches tall. The next time, it had grown another 55 inches. How tall was Dylan's sunflower?

    _____

7. Mr. Washington mailed 3 packages. The first was 6 pounds, the second was 11 pounds, and the third was 14 pounds. How much did his packages weigh in all?

    _____

DAY 7

Will the figures stack flat on top of each other? Circle *yes* or *no*.

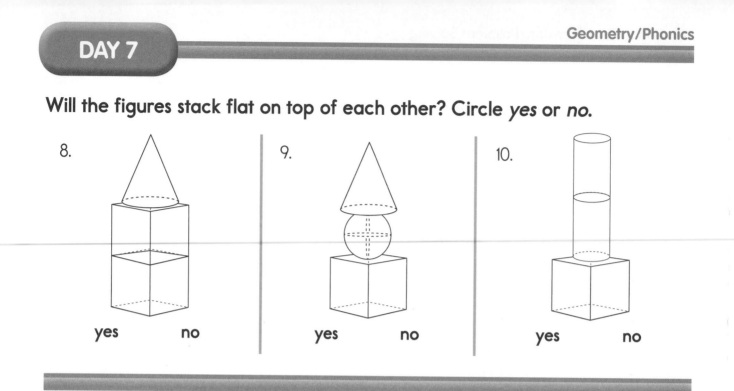

8.

yes   no

9.

yes   no

10.

yes   no

Read each word. Write *e* if the *y* makes the long *e* sound, as in *story*. Write *i* if the *y* makes the long *i* sound, as in *sky*.

11. ☐ baby   ☐ fly   ☐ windy   ☐ bunny   ☐ fry

12. ☐ shy   ☐ family   ☐ buy   ☐ happy   ☐ jelly

13. ☐ cry   ☐ my   ☐ funny   ☐ silly   ☐ try

FITNESS FLASH: Do 10 squats.

* See page ii.

PLACE STICKER HERE

Circle the word in each row that does not belong.

1. bean   carrot   book   lettuce   peas

2. train   jet   leg   car   boat

3. cat   orange   green   blue   red

4. lake   ocean   pond   chair   river

5. bear   apple   lion   wolf   tiger

6. Jane   Kathy   Tom   Jill   Anna

7. park   scared   happy   sad   mad

8. tulip   daffodil   rose   daisy   basket

Write *oi* or *oy* to complete each word. Write the word on the line.

9. b_____ _____

10. t_____ _____

11. s_____ _____l

12. p_____ _____nt

13. _____ _____ster

14. v_____ _____ce

FACTOID: If a cranberry is ripe, it will bounce.
Cranberries are also called bounceberries!

DAY 8

Read the story. Answer the questions.

Flying High

Ethan is a baby bald eagle. He is learning to fly. It has been a **struggle** for Ethan. He has been practicing for days, but he is not improving.

Getting up in the air is easy. Flying over fields is no problem. But, Ethan has trouble flying around things. He does not do well when he **attempts** to land on a certain spot. Perhaps he should sign up for flying lessons to improve his flying skills.

15. The word **struggle** means:

    A. something that is not easy

    B. a boat

    C. a broken wing

16. The word **attempts** means:

    A. sings

    B. tries

    C. waits

17. Learning to fly is hard for Ethan. How does he handle it?

_____

_____

_____

PLACE STICKER HERE

Write the correct verb to complete each sentence.

1. Amelia _____ a song.

    sing   sang

2. Did the bell _____ yet?

    ring   rang

3. The grass _____ green.

    is   are

4. She _____ a race.

    run   ran

5. Mom will _____ a short trip.

    took   take

6. Chris _____ a new scooter.

    has   have

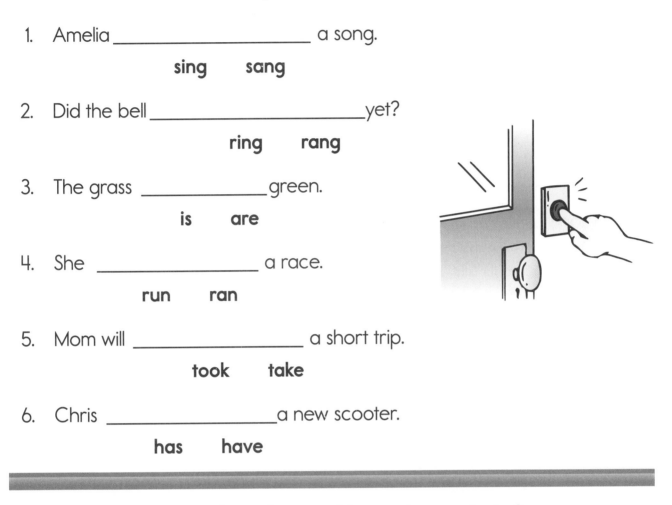

If you could plant a garden, what would you plant and why?

_____

_____

_____

_____

_____

_____

DAY 9

Solve each problem.

7. Cara spent 18¢. Danielle spent 10¢. How much did they spend altogether?

8. Pilar has 10 stamps. Edward has 15 stamps. How many stamps do they have altogether?

9. Nelan has 16 fish. Jay has 12 fish. How many fish do the two people have in all?

10. Emily has 13 balloons. Jessi has 10 balloons. How many balloons do they have in all?

Write words to fill the blanks.

Singular (One)	Plural (More Than One)
child	_____
mouse	_____
_____	feet
man	_____
_____	teeth
_____	people

PLACE STICKER HERE

Add to find each sum. Draw a line to match each dog with the correct bone.

1. 32
   +21

2. 73
   +24

3. 20
   +10

79

53

30

57

97

78

4. 44
   +13

5. 52
   +26

6. 61
   +18

Say the name of each picture. Circle the letters that make each ending sound.

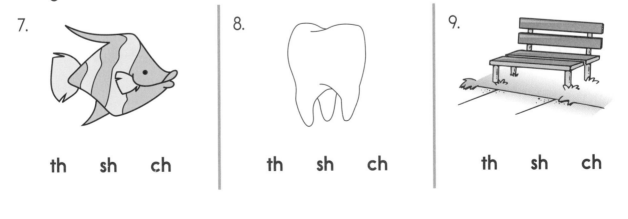

7.   th   sh   ch

8.   th   sh   ch

9.   th   sh   ch

DAY 10

Complete each number line.

Count by twos.

10.

2   4   6   ___   ___   ___

Count by fours.

11.

4   ___   12   ___   ___   ___

Count by fives.

12.

5   ___   15   ___   ___   30

Write a contraction from the word bank that means the same thing as each word pair does.

| we'll | it's | you'll | I'm | she'll | they've |

13. it is _____

14. they have _____

15. we will _____

16. I am _____

17. you will _____

18. she will _____

CHARACTER CHECK: Talk with an adult about the best time and way to ask for something.

PLACE STICKER HERE

Draw lines to divide each rectangle into rows and columns. Then, count how many squares there are. Write your answer on the line.

1. 3 rows
   4 columns

   How many squares?_____

2. 4 rows
   5 columns

   How many squares?_____

Have you ever helped someone without the person knowing? How did you feel?

_____

_____

_____

_____

_____

DAY 11

Rearrange the letters in the phrase *camping trip* to make new words. Write the words on the lines.

camping trip

_____

_____

_____

Draw a line to divide each compound word into two words. Write the words on the line.

3. goldfish

_____

4. popcorn

_____

5. daytime

_____

6. doghouse

_____

7. spaceship

_____

8. railroad

_____

9. blueberry

_____

10. sailboat

_____

11. grapefruit

_____

12. cupcake

_____

13. newspaper

_____

14. sometime

_____

FACTOID: Millions of trees are accidentally planted by squirrels because they forget where they hid the nuts!

PLACE STICKER HERE

Subtract to find each difference.

1. 10
   − 2

2. 10
   − 9

3. 10
   − 7

4. 10
   − 1

5. 10
   − 8

6. 10
   − 6

7. 10
   − 3

8. 11
   − 9

9. 11
   − 7

10. 11
    − 2

11. 11
    − 8

12. 11
    − 4

13. 11
    − 3

14. 12
    − 2

15. 12
    − 9

16. 12
    − 1

17. 12
    − 8

18. 12
    − 7

Write the time shown on each clock.

19.

____:____

20.

____:____

21.

____:____

22.

____:____

23.

____:____

24.

____:____

Number the sentences in the order that the events happened.

25. _____ Jenny made a chocolate cake for her friend.

26. _____ Jenny put blue frosting on the cake.

27. _____ Jenny put sprinkles on the cake.

28. _____ Jenny went to the store and bought a box of cake mix.

Draw and color a picture of the cake that Jenny made.

Integrity Issues

Integrity means that you always do the right thing, even when no one is watching. Having integrity is always doing what you feel is right whether you are in front of a group, with one person, or alone. On a separate sheet of paper, write what you would do in the following situation:

You helped start a school recycling program because you know that taking care of the earth is important. You are outside when you finish your granola bar. There is no trash can anywhere. What do you do with the wrapper?

FITNESS FLASH: Do 10 lunges.

* See page ii.

PLACE STICKER HERE

Choose the balloon whose number matches each description. Use the color listed to color the balloon.

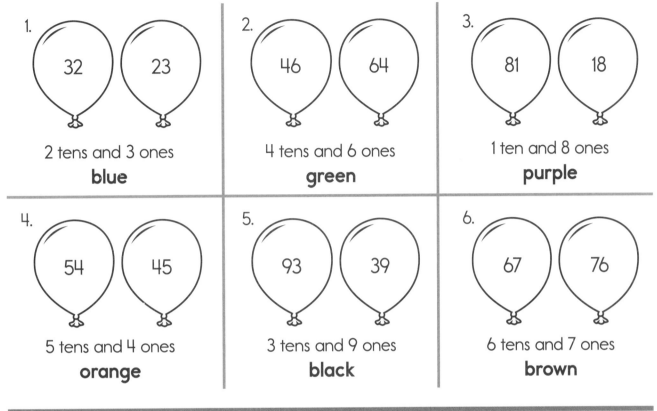

1.
32   23

2 tens and 3 ones
blue

2.
46   64

4 tens and 6 ones
green

3.
81   18

1 ten and 8 ones
purple

4.
54   45

5 tens and 4 ones
orange

5.
93   39

3 tens and 9 ones
black

6.
67   76

6 tens and 7 ones
brown

A noun followed by 's shows ownership. One noun in each sentence is missing an apostrophe.

Add it like this: Charlotte's kitty.

7. We stayed up late at Jonahs sleepover.

8. The cats fur is very soft.

9. Dantes cousin lives in Florida.

10. The maple trees leaves are changing color.

DAY 13

Read each sentence and circle each noun. A noun can be a person, place, or thing.

11. The boy lost his shoe.

12. She wrote a letter to her aunt.

13. Did you have a sandwich?

14. We saw a movie about butterflies.

15. My little sister has a shiny ring.

Write the months of the year in order.

October	March	February	April
December	July	November	June
August	May	January	September

_____   _____

_____   _____

_____   _____

_____   _____

_____   _____

_____   _____

FACTOID: Some types of bamboo can grow more than 40 in. (100 cm) per day.

PLACE STICKER HERE

Circle the odd numbers in each row.

1.	2	5	7	3	9	4	6	11	14
2.	1	10	6	7	12	13	15	2	17
3.	5	11	9	13	14	17	19	3	8

Circle the even numbers in each row.

4.	6	9	2	11	4	7	3	8	12
5.	13	8	10	6	12	16	9	5	19
6.	14	16	9	11	12	18	7	4	8

Read each word. Then, find a word in the box that has the same long-vowel spelling. Write it on the line.

pie	boat	sweet	throw	play	beach

7. green _____

8. cream _____

9. coat _____

10. lie _____

11. crow _____

12. may _____

DAY 14

Write the correct word to complete each sentence.

13. A dime is a _____ .

                 coin   coyn

14. I want to buy my friend a new _____ .

                                         toi   toy

15. My cat has one white_____ .

                           paw   pau

16. Dan has two sons and one_____ .

                           daughter   dawter

Invent and design a new kind of juice box. Draw your design below.
Describe your new juice box on a separate sheet of paper.

FITNESS FLASH: Do 10 squats.

* See page ii.

PLACE
STICKER
HERE

Read the passage. Answer the questions.

Black-Footed Ferrets

Years ago, many black-footed ferrets lived in the American West. They were wild and free. Their **habitat** was the flat grasslands. This habitat was destroyed by humans.

The ferrets began to **vanish.** Almost all of them died. Scientists worked to save the ferrets' lives. Now, the number of ferrets has increased.

1. Where did the black-footed ferrets live?

   _____

2. Who worked to save the ferrets? _____

   _____

3. What happened after scientists started to help the ferrets?

   _____

4. The word *habitat* means:

   A. a costume worn by ferrets

   B. a pattern of behavior

   C. a place where something lives

5. The word *vanish* means:

   A. to be born

   B. to disappear

   C. to clean one's home

DAY 15

Write the correct numbers to get the answer in each box.

6. 4 – _____ =

    3 + _____ =

    2 + _____ =

    3

7. 5 + _____ =

    2 + _____ =

    9 – _____ =

    6

8. 7 + _____ =

    _____ – 1 =

    _____ – 3 =

    8

9. _____ – 4 =

    8 – _____ =

    3 + _____ =

    5

Write the correct contractions.

10. cannot _____

11. I am _____

12. you are _____

13. do not _____

14. he is _____

15. I will _____

Write the two words in each contraction.

16. didn't _____

17. isn't _____

18. you've _____

19. she's _____

20. couldn't _____

21. we're _____

CHARACTER CHECK: Discuss with an adult what you think are the three most important qualities of a good friend.

PLACE STICKER HERE

Write *is* or *are* to complete each sentence.

1. We_____ going to town tomorrow.

2. This book _____ not mine.

3. Where _____a box of cereal?

4. Seals _____ fast swimmers.

5. _____ he planning to help?

6. _____ you going to the festival?

Write a sentence using *is*.

_____

Write a sentence using *are*.

_____

Write the correct punctuation mark at the end of each sentence. Use the marks (.), (!), or (?).

7. Are we going to the park_____

8. Look out for the ball_____

9. I know you can do it_____

10. Do bulls have horns on their heads_____

11. The girl on the bike is my sister _____

DAY 16

Subtract to find each difference.

12. 15
    − 4

13. 14
    − 2

14. 16
    − 8

15. 17
    − 3

16. 13
    − 4

17. 10
    − 4

18. 18
    − 7

19. 13
    − 6

20. 11
    − 9

21. 16
    − 5

Holidays and product names begin with a capital letter. Underline each letter that should be a capital three times (b).

22. On valentine's day, Dad cooked a fancy

     dinner for Mom.

23. At the grocery store, we bought two boxes of

     tasty crunch granola bars.

24. We'll be back from vacation on labor day.

25. Scout and Otis are almost out of chicken nibblers dog treats.

FACTOID: Slugs have four noses to help them smell chemicals in water.

PLACE STICKER HERE

Read each question. Circle the correct answer. Draw the shape in the box.

1. I have three sides and three angles.

    What am I?

    A. a quadrilateral

    B. a triangle

    C. a hexagon

2. I am a polygon. I have five equal sides and angles. What am I?

    A. a hexagon

    B. a cube

    C. a pentagon

3. I am a polygon. I have six equal sides and angles. What am I?

    A. a hexagon

    B. a cube

    C. a quadrilateral

4. I am a quadrilateral with four equal sides. My opposite sides and opposite angles are equal. What am I?

    A. a rhombus

    B. a triangle

    C. a pentagon

DAY 17

Add to find each sum.

5.	8	6.	2	7.	1	8.	6	9.	2	10.	9
	3		6		9		5		4		2
	5		4		2		1		3		3
	+ 2		+ 3		+ 2		+ 2		+ 4		+ 5

11.	3	12.	5	13.	6	14.	0	15.	4	16.	7
	4		7		1		6		2		8
	5		2		8		1		3		2
	+ 3		+ 1		+ 1		+ 4		+ 2		+ 3

Pronouns take the place of nouns. A *reflexive pronoun* is a special type of pronoun that ends in *–self* or *–selves*. Circle the reflexive pronoun in each sentence.

17. Rico and I gave ourselves half an hour to get ready.

18. The girls were proud of themselves for winning the game.

19. You know yourself better than anyone else does.

20. Josie tried to give herself a haircut when she was two!

21. I told myself not to be scared as I entered the dark room.

FITNESS FLASH: Do five push-ups.

* See page ii.

PLACE STICKER HERE

Draw a line to match the price of each toy with the correct amount of money.

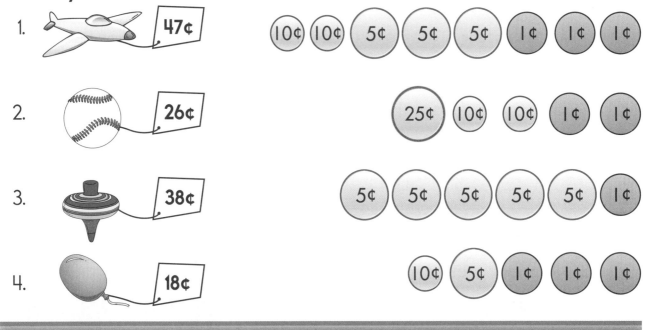

1. 47¢   10¢ 10¢ 5¢ 5¢ 5¢ 1¢ 1¢ 1¢

2. 26¢   25¢ 10¢ 10¢ 1¢ 1¢

3. 38¢   5¢ 5¢ 5¢ 5¢ 5¢ 1¢

4. 18¢   10¢ 5¢ 1¢ 1¢ 1¢

Draw a line to match each contraction on the left to the word pair on the right that makes the contraction.

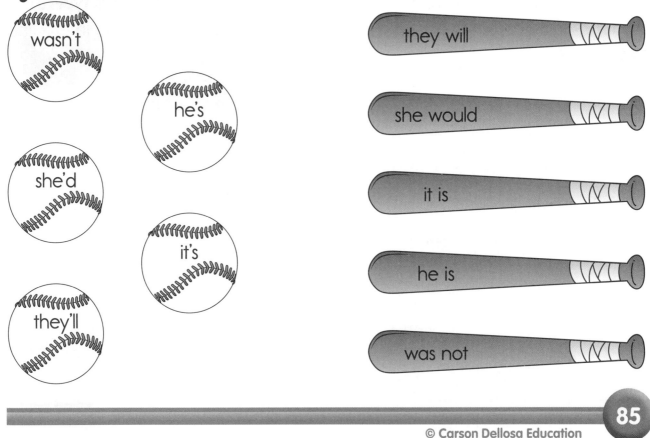

wasn't

he's

she'd

it's

they'll

they will

she would

it is

he is

was not

Mars

Have you ever dreamed of going to Mars? Mars is the fourth planet from the sun. A mineral gives the **surface** of Mars a red color. That's why it is called the *Red Planet.*

A day on Mars is about the same length as it is on Earth. Mars has seasons, too. They last longer than Earth's seasons. This is because Mars is farther from the sun. It is much colder there. A summer day on Mars would feel like an icy cold winter day on Earth!

5. Why is Mars called the *Red Planet?*

   A. No one knows for sure.

   B. A mineral gives it a red color.

   C. The air on Mars is red.

6. What does *surface* mean?

   A. the top of

   B. the bottom of

   C. instead of

7. Why did the author write this passage?

   A. to tell a funny story about Mars

   B. so people would move to Mars

   C. to give some facts about Mars

FACTOID: The Sahara desert covers 3.5 million square miles (9 million square km) or about one-third of Africa.

PLACE STICKER HERE

Write the best adjective from the word bank to complete each sentence. An adjective is a word that describes a person, place, or thing.

| funny | furry | hard | oak | red | six |

1. His kite got caught in that _____ tree.

2. I cannot believe you ate _____ apples.

3. We laughed at the _____ clowns.

4. Kayley got a _____ bike from her parents.

5. My pillow is very _____ and lumpy.

6. The rabbits all have soft and _____ ears.

Circle the main idea of each picture.

7.

   A. The boy gives his sister a balloon today.

   B. The boy is young.

8.

   A. The children are wearing funny masks.

   B. The children are standing next to each other.

DAY 19

Circle the coins that add up to the amount shown.

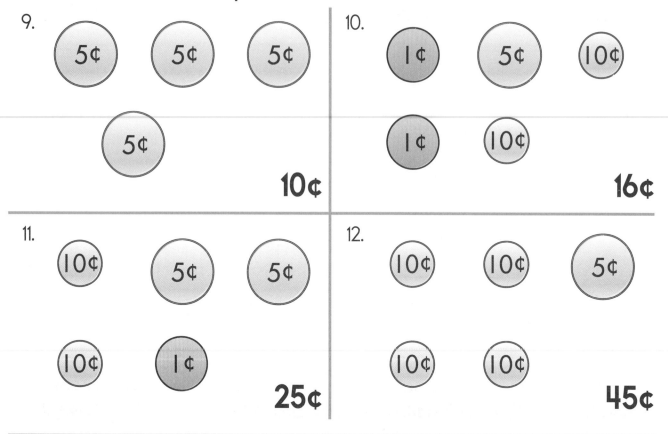

9.

5¢   5¢   5¢

5¢

10¢

10.

1¢   5¢   10¢

1¢   10¢

16¢

11.

10¢   5¢   5¢

10¢   1¢

25¢

12.

10¢   10¢   5¢

10¢   10¢

45¢

Write the meaning of each word. Use the meanings of the prefixes to help you.

un– = not	dis– = not, opposite of
re– = again	pre– = before

13.   unsafe = _____

14.   rebuild = _____

15.   dislike = _____

16.   precook = _____

PLACE
STICKER
HERE

Solve each problem.

1. $\begin{array}{r} 10 \\ -\ 4 \\ \hline \end{array}$

2. $\begin{array}{r} 18 \\ -14 \\ \hline \end{array}$

3. $\begin{array}{r} 7 \\ -3 \\ \hline \end{array}$

4. $\begin{array}{r} 7 \\ +5 \\ \hline \end{array}$

5. $\begin{array}{r} 8 \\ +2 \\ \hline \end{array}$

6. $\begin{array}{r} 6 \\ -4 \\ \hline \end{array}$

7. $\begin{array}{r} 9 \\ -4 \\ \hline \end{array}$

8. $\begin{array}{r} 11 \\ -\ 1 \\ \hline \end{array}$

9. $\begin{array}{r} 11 \\ +\ 8 \\ \hline \end{array}$

10. $\begin{array}{r} 10 \\ -\ 8 \\ \hline \end{array}$

11. $8 + 6 =$ _____

12. $9 + 3 =$ _____

13. $4 + 9 =$ _____

Use a ruler to measure the nails in inches. Then, show the measurements on the line plot. For each nail, draw an X above the number that shows its correct measurement.

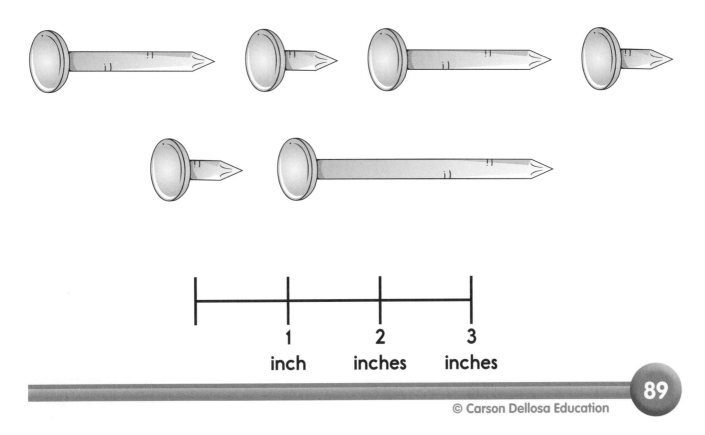

1	2	3
inch	inches	inches

DAY 20

Read each sentence. Follow the directions.

Draw a plate on a place mat.

Draw a napkin on the left side of the plate.

Draw a fork on the napkin.

Draw a knife and spoon on the right side of the plate.

Draw a glass of juice above the knife and spoon.

Draw your favorite lunch on the plate.

Complete the writing activity.

If I could fly anywhere, I would fly to _____ because

_____

_____

_____

_____

_____

CHARACTER CHECK: Gather your outgrown gently-used toys and books and give them to a local shelter.

PLACE STICKER HERE

Super Sediment

What sinks to the bottom of a river first—soil, sand, or pebbles?

Materials:
- 3 paper cups
- funnel
- pebbles
- soda bottle (2-liter with cap)
- sand
- soil
- water

Procedure:

1. Fill one paper cup with soil, one cup with sand, and one cup with pebbles. These will be the sediment.

2. Use the funnel to pour the soil, sand, and pebbles into the bottle. Pour water into the bottle until it is almost full. Close the cap tightly.

3. Shake the bottle until everything is mixed well.

4. Place the bottle on a table. On a separate sheet of paper, draw a picture of what you see in the bottle. Watch as the sediment begins to settle in the bottle.

5. Check the bottle after 15–30 minutes. Draw what you see.

6. Check the bottle again in 24 hours. Draw what you see.

What's This All About?

Sediment is the soil, sand, and pebbles that wash into streams, rivers, and lakes. In nature, sediment piles up and forms sedimentary rocks.

In the bottle, you have created a small body of water with a lot of sediment. The larger pieces of sediment settle to the bottom more quickly. The smaller pieces of sediment are more likely to float in the water longer and settle to the bottom more slowly.

Think About It

- What is a funnel? Why do you need to use one to get the materials into the bottle?

- Which section of the experiment tells you what to do, step by step?

* See page ii.

BONUS

Sweet, Sour, Salty, Bitter

Did you know that you can make a taste map of your tongue?

Materials:
- lemon (cut in half)
- pretzel
- water
- grapefruit rind
- sugar cube

Procedure:

1. Touch the inside of a lemon to the very tip of your tongue. Do you taste it? Don't move your tongue around. Rinse your mouth with water. Touch the lemon to the middle of your tongue. Do you taste it? Rinse your mouth with water. Touch the lemon to the sides of your tongue. Do you taste it?

2. Rinse your mouth with water. Repeat the activity with the pretzel, the grapefruit, and finally the sugar cube.

What's This All About?

There are four main tastes that humans can tell apart: sweet, sour, salty, and bitter. Your tongue is divided into different taste zones. Each taste zone is a certain area of your tongue. In this activity, you should discover which parts of your tongue detect each kind of taste.

More Fun Ideas to Try:

Based on your experiment, draw a taste map of your tongue. First, draw a picture of your tongue in the box. Then, label each area where you tasted salty, sweet, sour, and bitter.

* See page ii.

Look What I Did!

A time line is a list of dates that tells important things that have happened. You have already had a lot of things happen in your lifetime. Make a time line to show your accomplishments, milestones, and important events. Ask an adult to help you. If you have a baby book, scrapbooks, photo albums, or other records, use those things to help, too. You will need a piece of poster board and markers to create the time line. List at least 10 different events to show a variety of activities. If possible, attach photos or drawings to highlight the events. This is a fun way to look back at your history. Display the time line in a special place in your bedroom. Add to it as you grow and do more.

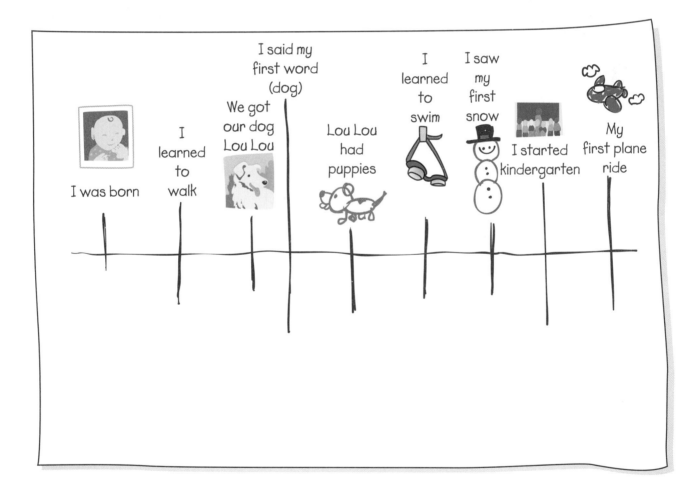

BONUS

Sandbox Relief Map

Some maps help people find their way. Other maps show physical features (things like oceans and mountains) of places. These are called relief maps. Make your own relief map in a sandbox. Get out your shovel and pail to dig and build. Be sure to make features such as a mountain, a lake, a river, a hill, an ocean, an island, a volcano, a desert, a forest, and a valley. Add water to fill up the water features. Use things that you find in nature, such as rocks, to build the mountains. Find some small sticks for trees and bushes. Soon, you will have your own real-life relief map.

* See page ii.

Having a Ball on Earth

A globe is a 3-D map that shows what Earth looks like. Make your own globe with a beach ball or large plastic ball and markers. Draw a line around the middle of the ball to represent the equator. The equator is a pretend line that marks the middle of the world. Label the top of the ball *north pole* and the bottom of the ball *south pole*. The north and south poles are places that mark the top and the bottom of Earth. Draw and label the seven continents (Africa, Antarctica, Asia, Australia, Europe, North America, and South America) and the four major oceans (Arctic, Atlantic, Indian, and Pacific). Place a star sticker on the globe to represent the place where you live. Toss the globe around with a friend or family member, and try to learn the names of the important places that you marked. Soon, you will know more about Earth than you did before.

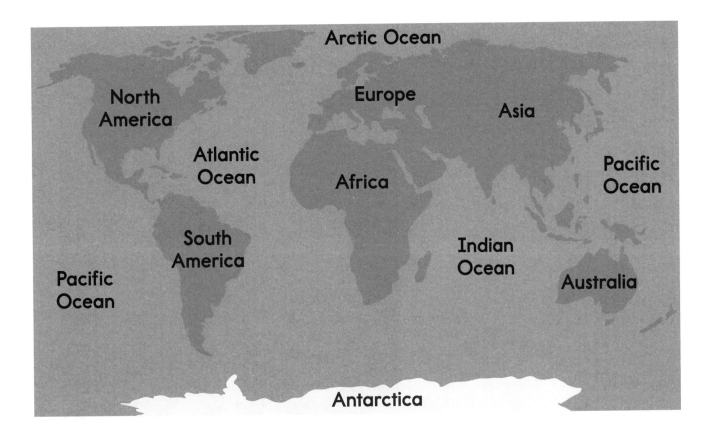

BONUS

Take It Outside!

Set up a safe, mini-obstacle course in a grassy area. Use soft objects, such as piles of cut grass or piles of leaves. Arrange the items in a line. When you reach the end of the course, turn around and retrace your steps to repeat it. Vary the way that you go through the course, such as running, hopping, crabwalking, or skipping.

Take a friend, sibling, or parent outside with you and challenge him to a "rhyme-off." Find a spot to sit down and begin by pointing out an object that you see, such as a rose. Invite your partner to think of a real word that rhymes with *rose*, such as *nose*. (*Zose* will not work.) Go back and forth until neither of you can think of any other rhyming words. Then, pick a new outside word and start again.

Play outdoor opposites. The park is perfect for this game. While you're there, look around. Try to find opposite events that are happening. For example, you might see a sad toddler who fell when playing and a happy dog rolling in the grass. See how many opposites you can find!

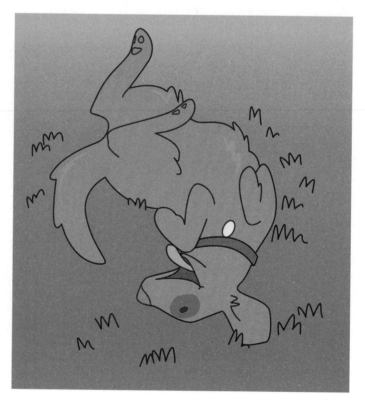

* See page ii.

Monthly Goals

Think of three goals to set for yourself this month. For example, you may want to do 30 math problems in one minute. Have an adult help you write your goals on the lines.

Place a sticker next to each of your goals that you complete. Feel proud that you have met your goals!

1. _____ PLACE STICKER HERE

2. _____ PLACE STICKER HERE

3. _____ PLACE STICKER HERE

Word List

The following words are used in this section. They are good words for you to know. Read each word aloud with an adult. When you see a word from this list on a page, circle it with your favorite color of crayon.

cause	hundred
collect	map
effect	opinion
energy	subtract
fact	sum

Introduction to Endurance

This section includes fitness and character development activities that focus on endurance. These activities are designed to get your child moving and to get her thinking about developing her physical and mental stamina.

Physical Endurance

Many children seem to have endless energy and can run, jump, and play for hours. But, other children may not have developed that kind of endurance. Improving endurance requires regular aerobic exercise, which causes the heart to beat faster and the person to breathe harder. As a result of regular aerobic activity, the heart becomes stronger, and the blood cells deliver oxygen to the body more efficiently. There are many ways for a child to get an aerobic workout that does not feel like exercise. Jumping rope and playing tag are examples.

Summer provides a variety of opportunities to bolster your child's endurance. If you see your child head for the TV, suggest an activity that will get her moving instead. Explain that while there are times when a relaxing indoor activity is valuable, it is important to take advantage of the warm mornings and sunny days to go outdoors. Reserve the less active times for when it is dark, too hot, or raining. Explain the importance of physical activity, and invite her to join you for a walk, a bike ride, or a game of basketball.

Endurance and Character Development

Endurance applies to the mind as well as to the body. Explain to your child that *endurance* means to stick with something. Children can demonstrate mental endurance every day. For example, staying with a task when she might want to quit and keeping at it until it is done are ways that a child can show endurance.

Take advantage of summertime to help your child practice her mental endurance. Look for situations where she might seem frustrated or bored. Perhaps she asked to take swimming lessons, but after a few early-morning classes, she is not having as much fun as she had imagined. Turn this dilemma into a learning opportunity. It is important that children feel some ownership in decision making, so guide her to some key points to consider, such as how she asked all spring for permission to take lessons. Remind her that she has taken only a few lessons, so she might get used to the early-morning practices. Let her know that she has options to make the experience more enjoyable, such as going to bed earlier or sleeping a few extra minutes during the morning ride to lessons. Explain that quitting should be the last resort. Teaching your child at a young age to endure will help her as she continues to develop into a happy, healthy person.

Complete each table.

1.

Add 10	
5	15
8	
7	
9	
3	
4	

2.

Add 8	
2	
6	
4	
7	
3	
5	

3.

Add 6	
10	
6	
8	
7	
4	
5	

Circle the word that is spelled correctly in each row.

4. ca'nt   can'nt   can't

5. esy   easy   eazy

6. kea   key   kee

7. buy   buye   biy

8. liht   light   ligte

9. wonce   onse   once

10. carry   carey   carre

11. you're   yure   yo're

12. star   stor   starr

13. funy   funny   funnie

Read the story. Then, answer the questions.

Once, there were two frogs who lived in a marsh. On a very hot summer day, the marsh dried up. The frogs had to look for another place to live. After some time, they found a deep well. "What a nice, cool, damp spot," said one frog. "Let us jump in and make ourselves at home."

The other frog was wiser. "Not so fast, dear friend. What if this well dries up like the marsh? How would we ever get out again?"

14. What is the moral of this story?
    A. A penny saved is a penny earned.
    B. Look before you leap.
    C. Slow and steady wins the race.

15. What is the point of a fable?
    A. to teach a lesson
    B. to change the reader's mind about something
    C. to give directions

Write each word from the word bank under the word that has the same vowel sound.

coat	drove	fox	job
rock	rope	those	top

nose

pop

_____   _____

_____   _____

_____   _____

_____   _____

Complete each table.

1.

Subtract 5	
9	4
5	
7	
10	
11	
8	

2.

Subtract 3	
10	
9	
7	
8	
6	
11	

3.

Subtract 2	
11	
7	
9	
5	
8	
6	

Combine each pair of sentences into a compound sentence. Use the conjunction in parentheses ( ). Make sure to put a comma before each conjunction.

EXAMPLE: Malik mowed the yard. He didn't weed the garden. (but)
        Malik mowed the yard, but he didn't weed the garden.

4.   Jackson made a fruit salad. Lena brought dessert. (and)

   _____

5.   The bunny hopped across the yard. The cat did not see it. (but)

   _____

6.   I could hear the rain on the roof. I knew the storm had begun. (so)

   _____

7.   Julia walks to school with Chase. She rides the bus. (or)

   _____

DAY 2

Use the mileage maps to answer the questions.

8. How many miles is it from Salt Lake City to Bountiful? _____

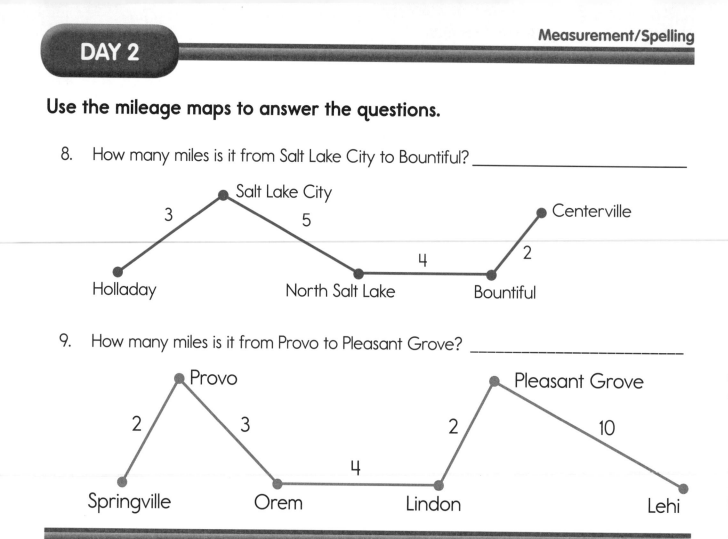

9. How many miles is it from Provo to Pleasant Grove? _____

Read each sentence. If the underlined word is spelled correctly, circle *yes*. If the underlined word is not spelled correctly, circle *no*.

10.	Uma is a very <u>brav</u> girl.	yes	no
11.	The United States flag is red, white, and <u>bloo</u>.	yes	no
12.	Those girls were in my <u>class</u>.	yes	no
13.	Gina is a very <u>helpfull</u> friend.	yes	no
14.	I turned off the <u>light</u>.	yes	no
15.	This glue is sticky <u>stuf</u>.	yes	no
16.	Is <u>shee</u> coming with us?	yes	no

FITNESS FLASH: Do 10 jumping jacks.

* See page ii.

PLACE STICKER HERE

Add to find each sum.

1. 29
    +12

2. 28
    +43

3. 67
    +26

4. 42
    +39

5. 89
    +11

6. 76
    +24

7. 66
    +24

8. 91
    + 9

9. 58
    +33

10. 46
    +16

Measure each item in centimeters. Then, answer the questions.

11.

How long is the alligator? _____

How long is the saw? _____

How much longer is the alligator than the saw? _____

12.

How long is the guitar? _____

How long is the violin? _____

How much longer is the guitar than the violin? _____

DAY 3

Count the hundreds, tens, and ones. Write the number.

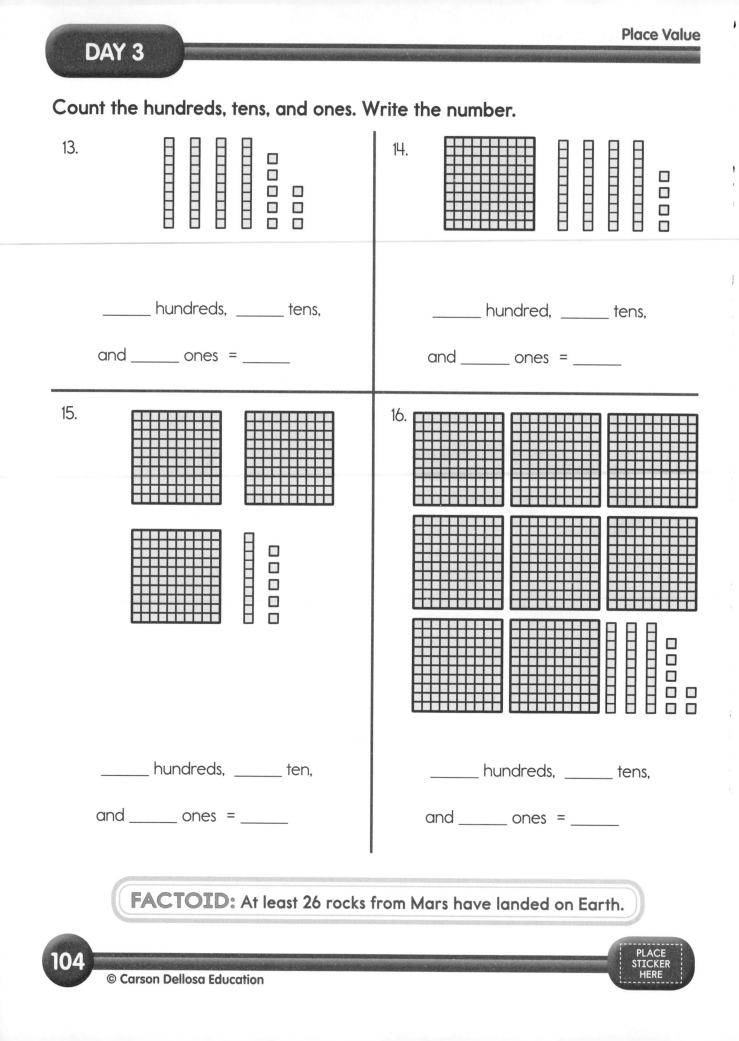

13.

_____ hundreds, _____ tens,

and _____ ones = _____

14.

_____ hundred, _____ tens,

and _____ ones = _____

15.

_____ hundreds, _____ ten,

and _____ ones = _____

16.

_____ hundreds, _____ tens,

and _____ ones = _____

FACTOID: At least 26 rocks from Mars have landed on Earth.

PLACE
STICKER
HERE

Write the numeral for each number word.

1. nine hundred ninety-six _____
2. twenty-one _____
3. eighty-two _____
4. thirty-seven _____
5. two hundred sixty-five _____
6. six hundred sixty-one _____
7. seventy-nine _____
8. fifty-eight _____
9. twenty-two _____
10. seven hundred eighty _____
11. one hundred eighteen _____
12. one hundred _____

Solve each problem. Write your answer on the line.

13. Silas is 54 inches tall. Lily is 8 inches shorter than he is. How tall is Lily?

    _____

14. Anton picked 18 sunflowers, Luis picked 14, and Lola picked 26. How many

    sunflowers did they pick in all? _____

15. Noah and Aylen are collecting canned food for a food drive. On Monday, they

    collected 56 cans. On Tuesday, they collected 36 cans. How many cans did they

    collect in all? _____

16. Kris saved up $45. He decided to buy a skateboard for $27. How much money did

    he have left? _____

DAY 4

Read the poem.

My Cat

Have you seen my cat?
Yes, I've seen your cat.

Really? My cat is big.
I saw a big cat.

My cat has spots.
I saw a big cat with spots.

My cat's spots are black.
I saw a big cat with black spots.

My cat runs fast.
I saw a big cat with black spots running fast.

You did see my cat! Where is it?
I don't know. I saw it last week.

Draw a line to connect each word with its antonym.

17. big   black

18. slow   little

19. white   fast

Answer the questions.

20. What is the poem about? _____

21. Describe the cat. _____

_____

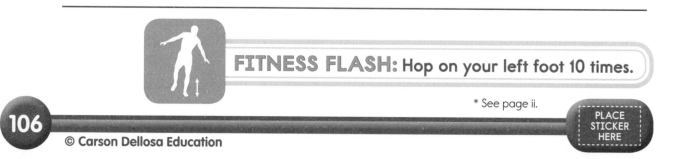

FITNESS FLASH: Hop on your left foot 10 times.

* See page ii.

PLACE STICKER HERE

Color the shape whose number matches each description.

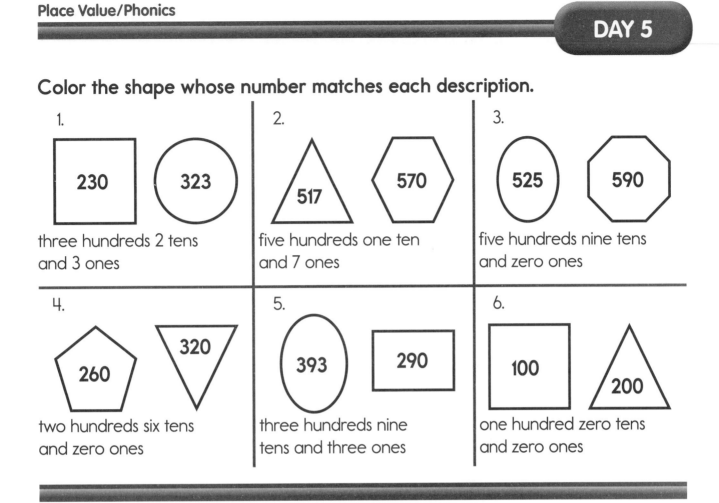

1.
230   323

three hundreds 2 tens and 3 ones

2.
517   570

five hundreds one ten and 7 ones

3.
525   590

five hundreds nine tens and zero ones

4.
320   260

two hundreds six tens and zero ones

5.
393   290

three hundreds nine tens and three ones

6.
100   200

one hundred zero tens and zero ones

Write each word from the word bank under the word that has the same vowel sound.

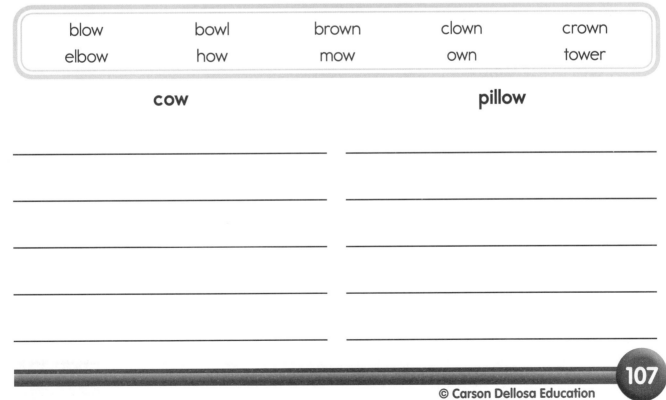

| blow | bowl | brown | clown | crown |
| elbow | how | mow | own | tower |

cow

pillow

_____   _____

_____   _____

_____   _____

_____   _____

DAY 5

Write the letter of each cause beside its effect.

Effects	Causes
7. _____ Justin put on his mittens.	A. It was cold outside.
8. _____ Chloe put ice in the water.	B. Her feet had grown.
9. _____ Ahmet gave his dog a bath.	C. The bike's tires were flat.
10. _____ Evan put air in his bike tires.	D. The rabbit was hungry.
11. _____ Kari got a new pair of shoes.	E. The water was warm.
12. _____ The rabbit ate the carrot.	F. The dog played in the mud.

Imagine that you are going on a trip. You can take only one thing. What would you take? Why?

_____

_____

_____

_____

CHARACTER CHECK: Make a list of things you can do to show respect to animals.

PLACE
STICKER
HERE

Circle the correct rule for each number pattern.

1.

2, 4, 6, 8, 10, 12

+2   +1

2.

20, 18, 16, 14, 12, 10

–2   –3

3.

50, 60, 70, 80, 90, 100

–10   +10

4.

80, 79, 78, 77, 76, 75

+10   –1

Tell about a time when you were worried about trying something new. What did you do? How did you feel afterward?

_____

_____

_____

_____

_____

DAY 6

Read the passage. Answer the questions.

Stamp Collecting

Are you a **philatelist**? If you collect stamps, that is what you are! Stamp collecting is a fun and interesting hobby.

If you want to start collecting stamps, you will need a few supplies. You will need a pair of tweezers to move the stamps so that they do not get dirty. You will also need an album with plastic pages to store your stamps.

Start by collecting some stamps. The stamps you collect can be new or used. You can collect stamps from letters that are delivered to your house. You can also buy stamps to add to your collection.

Next, decide how to sort your stamps. You can group them by their value, by the places they are from, or by the types of pictures on them. Then, place the stamps in your album.

Keep your stamp album in a cool, dry place away from direct sunlight. Heat, sun, and dampness can ruin your stamps.

5. Which sentence tells the main idea of the passage?

    A. Stamp collecting is a fun and interesting hobby.

    B. You can organize stamps in many different ways.

    C. Stamps come from all over the world.

6. What is a **philatelist**? _____

    _____

7. What is the main idea of the third paragraph?

    _____

8. Why did the author write this selection?

    _____

PLACE
STICKER
HERE

Write a number on each line to tell how many parts of the shape are colored.

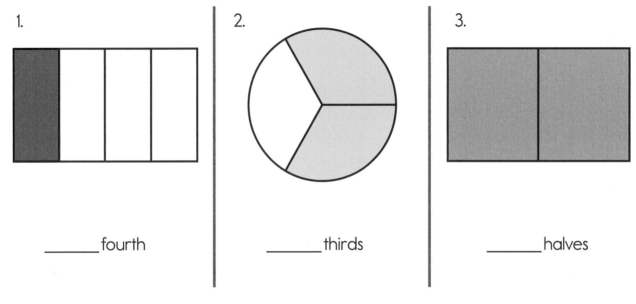

1.

_____fourth

2.

_____thirds

3.

_____halves

Complete each sentence with the correct compound word from the word bank.

cartwheel	fireworks	grandfather
snowflakes	sunflower	waterfall

4. The _____ lit up the night sky.

5. My mother's dad is my _____ .

6. In gym class, we learned how to do a _____ .

7. The _____ is a large, yellow flower.

8. When the first_____ fall, we know winter is coming.

9. We pitched our tent near a beautiful _____ .

DAY 7

Solve each problem. Circle the largest sum in each row.

10.   16 + 4 = _____   10 + 9 = _____   7 + 8 = _____   8 + 9 = _____

11.   8 + 8 = _____   13 + 6 = _____   9 + 9 = _____   5 + 7 = _____

12.   6 + 13 = _____   5 + 5 = _____   9 + 4 = _____   7 + 9 = _____

13.   8 + 3 = _____   12 + 2 = _____   4 + 15 = _____   6 + 7 = _____

Read the story. Circle each answer that makes sense. There may be more than one answer.

14.   Murphy's mom quickly pulled everything out of the dryer. Then, she lifted the lid of the washer, looked inside, and shook her head. She looked around the kitchen and family room, and then she rushed upstairs. "I cannot find it," she called to Murphy. "The last time I saw it was after the game on Saturday. We have to find it before 4:00!"

   A.   Murphy's mom has friends coming over at 4:00.

   B.   Murphy's mom is looking for Murphy's soccer jersey.

   C.   Murphy has a game today at 4:00.

   D.   Murphy's mom lost her purse.

FITNESS FLASH: Hop on your right foot for 30 seconds.

* See page ii.

PLACE STICKER HERE

Measure each object. Write the length in inches and in centimeters.

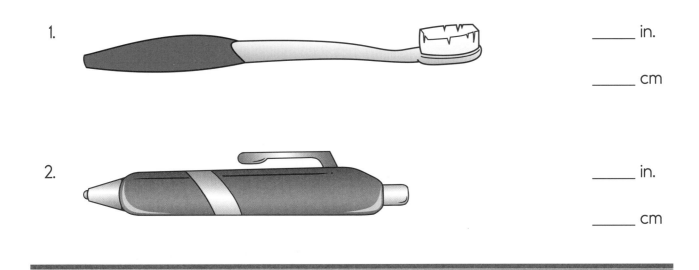

1. _____ in.

   _____ cm

2. _____ in.

   _____ cm

Jump for Joy and Fitness!

Build your endurance and have a hopping good time doing it! Grab a jump rope and find some happy music. Turn on the music and start jumping rope. See how long you can jump as you listen to your favorite songs. Rest in between songs based on your stamina. (*Stamina* just means your "staying power" or how long you can do something until you need a break.) If jumping rope is too difficult, you can still improve your endurance by jumping in place. In a few days, try again and see how many songs you can jump through. By the end of the summer, you may be able to jump through even more music, and your endurance will be better!

* See page ii.

DAY 8

Use the chart to answer each question.

Allowance for Each Chore Completed

Bundle newspapers for recycling	$0.25
Empty wastepaper baskets	$0.75
Put away groceries	$0.50
Wash the car	$2.00
Set the table	$1.00

3. Which chore pays the most money? _____

4. If Hugo sets the table for dinner every night this week, how much

   will he earn? _____

5. Davis bundled newspapers for recycling two times this week. How much money

   did he earn?_____

Read each statement. Write Y for yes or N for no beside each statement.

How a Snake Is Like a Turtle

6. _____Both have shells.

7. _____Both can be on land.

8. _____Both are reptiles.

9. _____Both have scales.

How a Bike Is Like a Truck

10. _____Both have tires.

11. _____Both need gas.

12. _____Both can be new.

13. _____Both have four wheels.

FACTOID: Yo-yos have ridden on at least two NASA spacecraft.

114

PLACE
STICKER
HERE

Follow the directions to color the shapes.

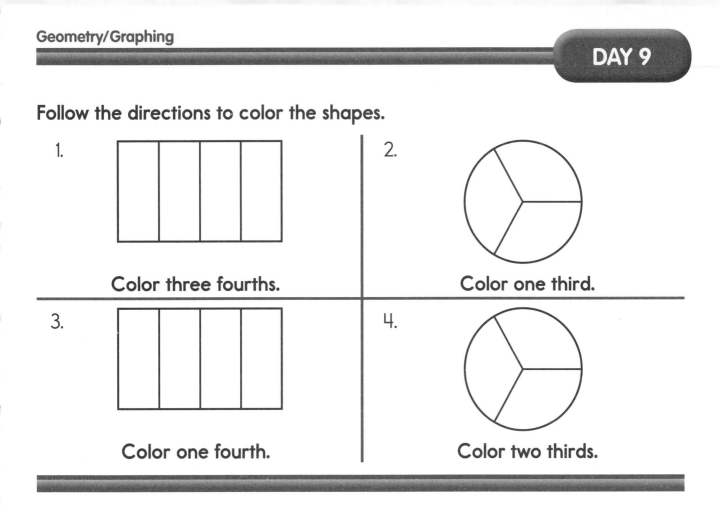

1.

Color three fourths.

2.

Color one third.

3.

Color one fourth.

4.

Color two thirds.

The bar graph shows concession stand sales at a baseball game. Use the bar graph to answer the questions.

5. Do people buy more nachos or

   fruit bowls?

   _____

6. How many more fruit bowls than

   pretzels were sold? _____

7. People bought more than 50 of

   which item?

   _____

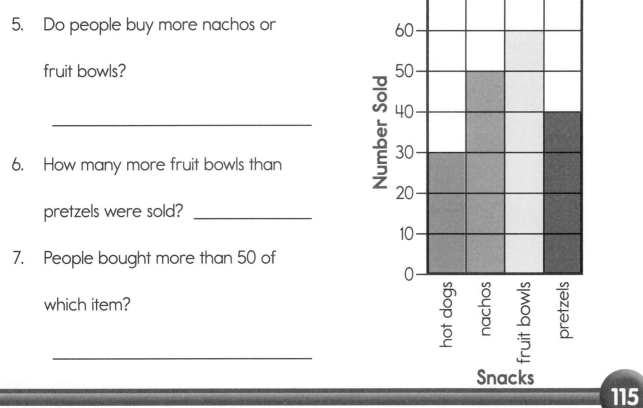

Concession Stand Sales

DAY 9

Solve each problem.

8. There are 26 students on one bus. There are 29 students on the other bus. How many students are on the buses altogether?

9. Nia found 47 shells on the beach. Byron found 44 shells on the beach. How many shells did they find in all?

10. Kamal ran 15 laps on Monday. He ran 17 laps on Tuesday. How many laps did Kamal run altogether?

11. Thomas saw 48 fish in one fish tank. Brooke saw 36 fish in another fish tank. How many fish did they see in all?

12. Write a sentence that ends with a period (.).

_____

13. Write a sentence that ends with a question mark (?).

_____

14. Write a sentence that ends with an exclamation point (!).

_____

FITNESS FLASH: Jog in place for 30 seconds.

* See page ii.

PLACE STICKER HERE

Use each fact family to write two addition and two subtraction number sentences.

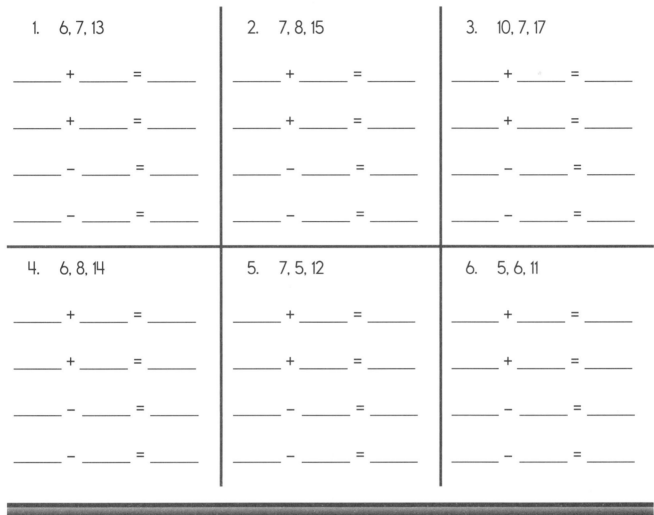

1. 6, 7, 13

_____ + _____ = _____

_____ + _____ = _____

_____ – _____ = _____

_____ – _____ = _____

2. 7, 8, 15

_____ + _____ = _____

_____ + _____ = _____

_____ – _____ = _____

_____ – _____ = _____

3. 10, 7, 17

_____ + _____ = _____

_____ + _____ = _____

_____ – _____ = _____

_____ – _____ = _____

4. 6, 8, 14

_____ + _____ = _____

_____ + _____ = _____

_____ – _____ = _____

_____ – _____ = _____

5. 7, 5, 12

_____ + _____ = _____

_____ + _____ = _____

_____ – _____ = _____

_____ – _____ = _____

6. 5, 6, 11

_____ + _____ = _____

_____ + _____ = _____

_____ – _____ = _____

_____ – _____ = _____

How many sentences can you write using only the words in the word bank? Write the sentences on a separate sheet of paper.

and	at	barks	bed	big	blue	boy
car	Dad	dog	girl	I	it	little
Mom	over	parks	ran	red	small	squirrel
the	to	tree	under	up	walks	yellow

DAY 10

Use the calendars to answer each question.

May						
S	M	T	W	Th	F	S
			1	2	3	4
5	6	7	8	9	10	11
12	13	14	15	16	17	18
19	20	21	22	23	24	25
26	27	28	29	30	31	

June						
S	M	T	W	Th	F	S
						1
2	3	4	5	6	7	8
9	10	11	12	13	14	15
16	17	18	19	20	21	22
23	24	25	26	27	28	29
30						

7. Julia went to the dentist on the third Tuesday in May. What was the date?

Tuesday, May _____

8. Heath started his dance class on the first Monday in June. What was the date?

Monday, June _____

9. Today is May 10. Adam's family will see a play next Thursday. On what date will they see a play?

Thursday, May _____

10. How many days are between May 29 and June 5?

_____

What do you think would be the most difficult part about being a parent?

_____

_____

_____

CHARACTER CHECK: Discuss with an adult how long you think it takes to regain someone's trust after telling a lie.

PLACE STICKER HERE

Write an addition equation to find the total number of items in each picture.

EXAMPLE:

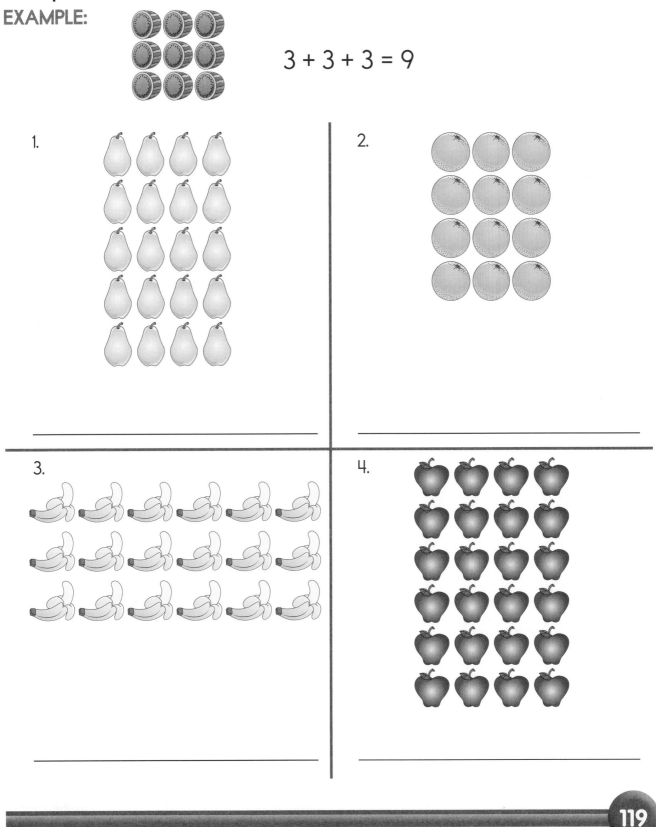

$3 + 3 + 3 = 9$

1.

2.

3.

4.

DAY 11

Some nouns name groups of people, animals, or things. Choose a noun from the box to complete each sentence.

class	family	school	herd

5. My _____ lives at 123 Maple Street.

6. We saw a _____ of cattle grazing in the field.

7. A _____ of fish swam under the dock.

8. On Wednesday, our _____ will take a field trip.

Use the words from the word bank to complete each analogy. An *analogy* is a way to show how things are alike. To complete an analogy, look at the first set of words. Decide how they are related. Apply that relationship to the second set of words.

EXAMPLE: *Finger : hand :: toe : _____.* (A *finger* is part of a *hand*. What is a *toe* a part of? The answer is *foot*.)

light	sky	square	table

9. sleep : bed :: eat : _____

10. three : triangle :: four : _____

11. green : grass :: blue : _____

12. win : lose :: dark : _____

FACTOID: Dragonflies can fly at speeds of up to 40 mph (64 km/h).

PLACE
STICKER
HERE

Solve each problem.

EXAMPLE:

Nick left for school on the bus at 8:00.   Think: 8:00 + 0:20 = 8:20
The bus ride took 20 minutes.
What time did Nick get to school?

1. Claire ate a snack at 10:00. She ate lunch 2 hours later. What time did she eat lunch?

_____

2. This morning, Hau read for 15 minutes. He started at 9:00. What time did he finish reading?

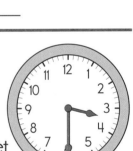

_____

3. Recess lasted 30 minutes. It started at 2:00. What time did it end?

_____

4. Ellis left school at 3:30. He rode the bus for 30 minutes. What time did he get off of the bus?

_____

Say each word aloud. Write the syllables in the boxes.

5. apartment   ☐ ☐☐☐☐ ☐☐☐☐

6. enormous   ☐ ☐☐☐☐ ☐☐☐☐

7. subtraction   ☐☐☐ ☐☐☐☐ ☐☐☐☐

8. wonderful   ☐☐☐ ☐☐☐ ☐☐☐

DAY 12

Solve each problem. Use the number line to help you add hundreds.

```
0   100  200  300  400  500  600  700  800  900  1,000
```

9. 300 + 200 = _____

10. 700 + 200 = _____

11. 100 + 200 = _____

12. 600 + 400 = _____

13. 400 + 400 = _____

14. 500 + 200 = _____

Read the table of contents. Write the chapter and page number where you should begin looking for the answer to each question.

Table of Contents

Chapter 1   Mammals (Animals with Fur) 3
Chapter 2   Reptiles (Snakes, Turtles, and Alligators) 13
Chapter 3   Amphibians (Frogs and Toads) 21
Chapter 4   Fish 35
Chapter 5   Insects and Spiders 49
Chapter 6   Birds 57

15. How long do lions live? Chapter _____ Page _____

16. How fast do sailfish swim? Chapter_____ Page _____

17. What color is a robin's egg? Chapter _____ Page _____

18. Do spiders bite? Chapter _____ Page _____

FITNESS FLASH: Do 10 jumping jacks.

* See page ii.

PLACE STICKER HERE

Read the story. Fill in the table.

Today is Rachel's birthday. She invited four friends to her party. Each friend brought a gift. Rachel's brother mixed up the tags on the gifts. Can you use the clues to put the tags on the correct gifts?

Grace's gift has flowered wrapping paper and a bow.

Kate's gift is small and has a bow.

Meghan forgot to put a bow on her gift.

Jade's gift has striped wrapping paper.

Write O in the box when you know a gift was brought by the girl.
Write X in the box when you know a gift was not brought by the girl.

Kate				
Grace				
Jade				
Meghan				

If you could give any gift in the world, what would you give? Whom would you give the gift to? Write your answers on a separate sheet of paper.

FACTOID: Some lungfish can survive out of the water for more than two years.

DAY 13

Read the story.

Aunt Antonym

We have a nickname for my mother's sister. We call her Aunt Antonym. She always says or does the opposite of what we say or do. One day, we all went to the zoo. At the monkey exhibit, we thought the monkeys were cute. My aunt thought that they were strange. Soon, we were hungry. My aunt was still full from breakfast. After lunch, we rode the train around the zoo. My aunt wanted to walk. Finally, my aunt said that she was tired and ready to go. We were still full of energy. We wished we could have stayed.

Write _T_ next to each statement that is true. Write _F_ next to each statement that is false.

1. _____ The author is writing about his sister.

2. _____ Aunt Antonym is the real name of the author's aunt.

3. _____ Aunt Antonym was full from breakfast.

4. _____ Aunt Antonym did not want to ride the train.

Write a word from the story that is an antonym for each word.

5. ride _____

6. stay _____

7. energetic _____

8. hungry _____

9. From whose point of view is the story told?

   A. Aunt Antonym

   B. Aunt Antonym's niece or nephew

   C. a monkey at the zoo

10. _Molly's Marvelous Mustards_ is an example of alliteration. What is an example of

    alliteration in this story? _____

Follow the directions to solve each problem.

1. Start with 800. Write the number that is 200 less. _____

2. Start with 600. Write the number that is 300 less. _____

3. Start with 200. Write the number that is 100 less. _____

4. Start with 700. Write the number that is 500 less. _____

5. Start with 900. Write the number that is 400 less. _____

6. Start with 600. Write the number that is 100 less. _____

Loyalty List

How can you show your loyalty this summer? Being loyal means supporting and standing up for those you love. What can you do to practice this important trait? Try making a

Loyalty List. Ask an adult for a large sheet of poster board and markers. Write the things that you will do to show loyalty to those you love, such as your family and friends. Then, decorate the poster board with pictures of your friends and family. With the adult's permission, place the poster on the wall or door in your bedroom. It will help you remember how you can be loyal every day. After a week, look at your Loyalty List and write examples of how you have shown your loyalty.

DAY 14

Complete each number pattern. Write the rule.

7. 2, 4, 6, 8,_____ ,_____ ,_____ ,_____ ,_____ ,_____

    Rule: _____

8. 10, 20, 30,_____ ,_____ ,_____ ,_____ ,_____ ,_____

    Rule: _____

9. 5, 10, 15,_____ ,_____ ,_____ ,_____ ,_____ ,_____

    Rule: _____

10. 3, 6, 9, 12,_____ ,_____ ,_____ ,_____ ,_____ ,_____

    Rule: _____

Pretend that you are planning a Silly Saturday party. Write a letter to invite someone to your party.

Dear _____ ,

_____

_____

_____

Your friend,

_____

FITNESS FLASH: Hop on your left foot 10 times.

* See page ii.

PLACE STICKER HERE

Repeated addition problems help you get ready for multiplication. Add to find each sum.

1. 3
    3
    + 3

2. 2
    2
    + 2

3. 4
    4
    + 4

4. 5
    5
    + 5

5. 3
    3
    3
    + 3

6. 2
    2
    2
    + 2

7. 5
    5
    5
    + 5

8. 4
    4
    4
    + 4

A *glossary* is found at the back of a book. It tells what certain words in the book mean. Use this glossary from a book about deserts to answer the questions below.

arid something that is very dry
camouflage coloring that helps an animal hide
desert an environment where very little rain falls; home to few plants and animals
evaporate to change from a liquid into a gas
precipitation any kind of water that falls from the sky (like rain, snow, hail, etc.)

9. What does *evaporate* mean? _____

10. A moth that blends in with the bark on a tree is using _____ .

11. If a place is arid, it is very _____ .

12. What is one example of precipitation? _____

DAY 15

Write the expanded form for each number.
EXAMPLE:

251 = __2__ hundreds + __5__ tens + __1__ one = **200** + **50** + __1__

13. 341 = _____ hundreds + _____ tens + _____ one = _____ + _____ + _____

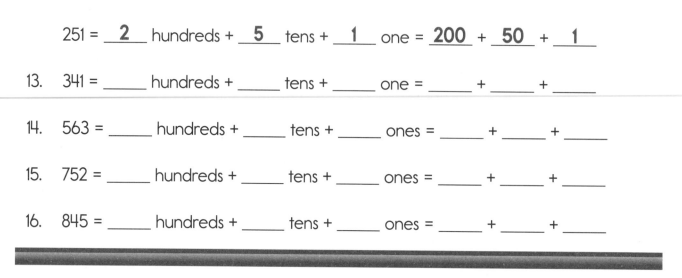

14. 563 = _____ hundreds + _____ tens + _____ ones = _____ + _____ + _____

15. 752 = _____ hundreds + _____ tens + _____ ones = _____ + _____ + _____

16. 845 = _____ hundreds + _____ tens + _____ ones = _____ + _____ + _____

Use the number line to help you solve each problem. Mark the number line to show your work.

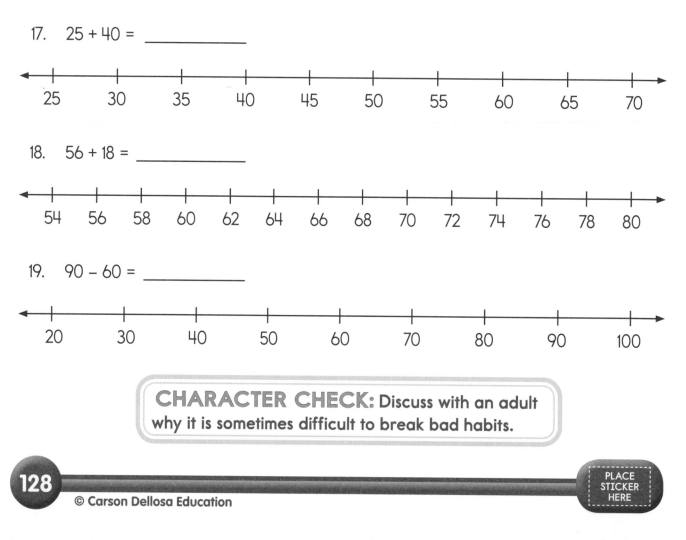

17. 25 + 40 = _____

| 25 | 30 | 35 | 40 | 45 | 50 | 55 | 60 | 65 | 70 |

18. 56 + 18 = _____

| 54 | 56 | 58 | 60 | 62 | 64 | 66 | 68 | 70 | 72 | 74 | 76 | 78 | 80 |

19. 90 – 60 = _____

| 20 | 30 | 40 | 50 | 60 | 70 | 80 | 90 | 100 |

CHARACTER CHECK: Discuss with an adult why it is sometimes difficult to break bad habits.

PLACE STICKER HERE

Read the passage. Answer the questions.

How Plants Grow

A plant needs **energy** to grow. Energy comes from food. A plant makes its food in its leaves. Sunlight and water help the plant make food. After you plant a seed, a tiny seedling pushes its way out from the soil. The plant grows toward the sun. The plant must get water, or it will dry out and die. The roots of the plant pull water and nutrients from the soil. If there is little rain where you live, you may need to water your plant. If the soil in your area has few nutrients, you may need to add plant food to the soil. That way your plant gets what it needs.

1. What is the main idea of this passage?

    A. A plant can die without water.

    B. Plants need food, water, and sunlight to grow.

    C. Plants start as seeds.

2. What happens after you plant a seed? _____

    _____

3. Where does energy come from? _____

    _____

4. When might you need to water your plant? _____

    _____

5. Why is the word *energy* in bold print in the passage? _____

    _____

DAY 16

Write *a* or *an* in front of each noun.

6. _____ mayor

7. _____ officer

8. _____ doctor

9. _____ scientist

10. _____ athlete

11. _____ explorer

12. _____ artist

Circle the adjective that describes each underlined noun.

13. Insects have six <u>legs</u>.

14. Bumblebees have hairy <u>bodies</u>.

15. A beetle has a hard <u>body</u>.

16. Ladybugs have black <u>spots</u>.

17. Butterflies can be beautiful <u>colors</u>.

18. Termites have powerful <u>jaws</u>.

19. Dragonflies have four <u>wings</u>.

20. A green <u>grasshopper</u> jumps away.

FACTOID: Butterflies and moths are found on every continent except Antarctica.

PLACE STICKER HERE

Write > (greater than) or < (less than) to compare each pair of numbers.

1. 103 ◯ 111

2. 640 ◯ 460

3. 322 ◯ 100

4. 190 ◯ 910

5. 290 ◯ 300

6. 985 ◯ 850

7. 140 ◯ 400

8. 124 ◯ 216

9. 648 ◯ 846

10. 680 ◯ 480

11. 592 ◯ 324

12. 745 ◯ 746

Wacky Walkathon

One of the best ways to build endurance is to walk. Grab some friends or family members and get going! Find a safe place, such as a park path, school track, or nature trail. Choose a date and invite your loved ones to join you for a wacky walkathon. To make it fun, have everyone arrive wearing a costume or funny face paint. Then, get your silly group walking. Remind them that they can have fun but that they must walk fast because they are exercising! Some people may not be able to walk for as long or as fast as everyone else. That is OK as long as each walker is doing his best. Try to get the group to meet for several walkathons to get fitter and even sillier as summer goes on!

* See page ii.

Look up the words in a dictionary. In each pair, circle the word that is misspelled. Write the word correctly on the line.

13. early   thougt   _____

14. caterpilar   scared   _____

15. sents   picnic   _____

16. because   dragin   _____

17. chane   while   _____

18. speshal   coat   _____

Read the story.

Winter Fun

Some people like spring, but I do not. I think that winter is the best season. My family goes to the mountains every year. My stepmom is a good skier. She skis while we watch. My dad wears snowshoes and goes on long walks. My brothers and I like to play in the snow. The nights are too cold to be outside. So, we stay warm in our cabin. My stepmom makes us hot chocolate at bedtime, and we tell stories.

Decide whether each sentence is a fact or an opinion. Write *F* for fact or *O* for opinion.

19. _____ Winter is the best season.

20. _____ My family goes to the mountains.

21. _____ My stepmom makes us hot chocolate.

22. _____ I think my stepmom is a good skier.

23. _____ The nights are too cold.

24. _____ Dad goes on long walks.

FITNESS FLASH: Hop on your right foot for 30 seconds.

* See page ii.

PLACE STICKER HERE

Read the passage. Answer the questions.

The Moon

The moon lights up the night sky. Sometimes, the moon looks narrow. Sometimes, it looks round. The appearance of the moon has to do with the position of the moon as viewed from Earth. When the moon is between the sun and Earth, the moon looks black. This is called a new moon. When Earth is between the sun and the moon, the moon looks bright and round. This is called a full moon. In the middle of these periods, half of the moon is lit, and half of the moon is dark. It takes about one month for the moon to finish the entire cycle.

1. What is the main idea of this passage?

   A. The moon can look thin or fat.

   B. The moon travels around Earth.

   C. The moon looks different throughout the month.

2. What makes the moon's appearance change? _____

   _____

3. When does a new moon happen?_____

   _____

4. When does a full moon happen?_____

   _____

5. What is the author's purpose for writing this passage?

   A. to tell facts about the moon's appearance

   B. to entertain the reader

   C. to encourage the reader to visit the moon

Estimate the length of each item in centimeters.
Then, measure to check your guess!

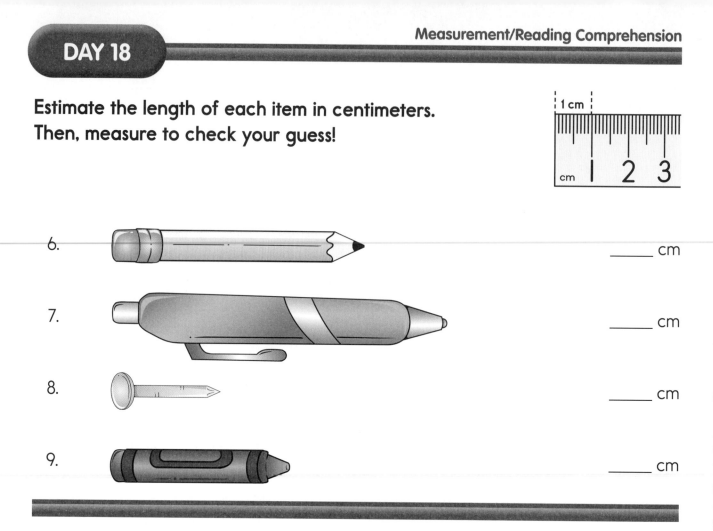

6. _____ cm

7. _____ cm

8. _____ cm

9. _____ cm

Read the story. Then, answer the questions.

Learning to Cook

My big brother is helping me learn to cook. I think he is an excellent cook. Last night, we made noodles with tomato sauce. We also made spinach bread. We planned to bake a pie, but we ran out of flour. Mom loved the meal. She said, "You boys are hired!"

10. Who is telling the story?

   A. the mother

   B. the older brother

   C. a boy who cooks with his big brother

11. Why didn't the boys bake a pie?_____

134

PLACE
STICKER
HERE

Read the passage. Answer the questions.

Teeth

Teeth are important for chewing food, so you need to take care of your teeth. When you are a child, you have baby teeth. These fall out and are replaced by adult teeth. You can expect to have 32 teeth one day. You should brush your teeth at least twice a day—once in the morning and once at bedtime. Also, you should floss to remove food that gets stuck between your teeth. That way, you will have a healthy smile!

1. What is the main idea of this passage?

    A. You can have a healthy smile.

    B. It is important to take care of your teeth.

    C. Adults have more teeth than children.

2. How does the author convince you to take good care of your teeth?

    _____

3. What happens to baby teeth?_____

    _____

4. How many teeth do adults have? _____

5. How often should you brush your teeth?

    A. only at lunchtime

    B. at least once a week

    C. at least twice a day

DAY 19

Subtract to find each difference.

6.	63 −40	7.	80 −60	8.	75 −50	9.	79 −20	10.	38 −10	11.	93 −30

12.	67 −40	13.	83 −20	14.	77 −10	15.	76 −50	16..	59 −30	17.	77 −60

Look up the words in a dictionary. Write the meanings on the lines.

18. **absorb:** _____

19. **drowsy:** _____

20. **victory:** _____

21. **lasso:** _____

22. **jostle:** _____

23. **overcast:** _____

24. **merchant:** _____

FITNESS FLASH: Jog in place for 30 seconds.

* See page ii.

PLACE STICKER HERE

Tara and her dad planted a tiny pine tree in their yard on her sixth birthday. They measured it every year on her birthday to see how many inches it had grown. Look at the graph and answer the questions.

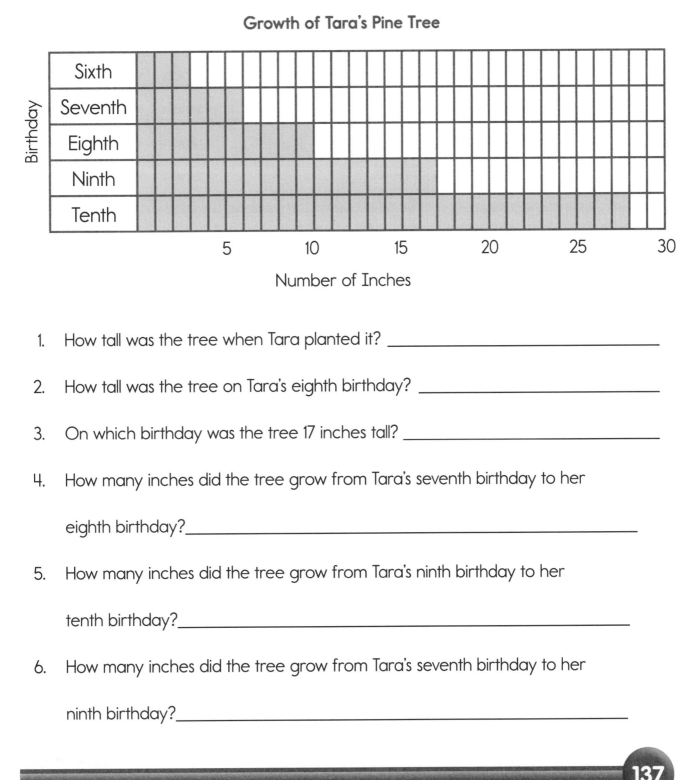

Growth of Tara's Pine Tree

1. How tall was the tree when Tara planted it? _____

2. How tall was the tree on Tara's eighth birthday? _____

3. On which birthday was the tree 17 inches tall? _____

4. How many inches did the tree grow from Tara's seventh birthday to her

   eighth birthday?_____

5. How many inches did the tree grow from Tara's ninth birthday to her

   tenth birthday?_____

6. How many inches did the tree grow from Tara's seventh birthday to her

   ninth birthday?_____

DAY 20

Adverbs often answer the questions *where, when,* or *how.* Underline the adverb in each sentence. Then, circle *when, where,* or *how* to show what question it answers.

7.   Mom and Dad clapped proudly for Shaun.   when   where   how

8.   Yuki called Grandma yesterday.   when   where   how

9.   Please take the puppy outside.   when   where   how

10. Will crossed the street safely.   when   where   how

11. Addy raced ahead of us.   when   where   how

12. I woke early to the chirps of birds.   when   where   how

Use the hundreds, tens, and ones blocks to help you solve each problem.

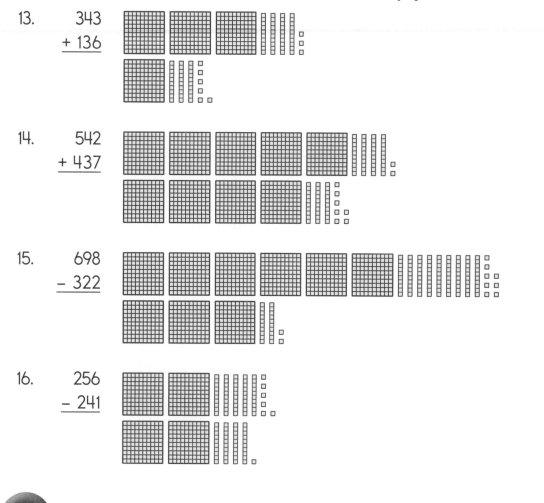

13.   343
     + 136

14.   542
     + 437

15.   698
     − 322

16.   256
     − 241

PLACE
STICKER
HERE

Catching Ice Cubes

Can you use salt and a piece of string to "catch" an ice cube?

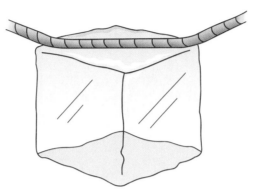

Materials:
- ice cube
- salt
- string

Procedure:
1. Try to catch the ice cube with the piece of string. (You cannot tie the string around the ice cube.) Can you do it?

2. Next, place the string on the ice cube and sprinkle a little salt on the string. Count to 30 and slowly lift the string. The ice cube will be attached!

What's This All About?

When you sprinkle salt on the ice, it lowers the freezing temperature of the ice. This causes some water to melt around the string. When the water forms, it **dilutes** the salt on the ice and allows the water to freeze around the string. This is why you can pick it up.

Think About It
- Why do you have to count to 30 before you lift the string?
- In the last paragraph, what do you think *dilutes* means?

Pinching Water

Can you hold two streams of water together? Or, can you separate two streams of water that had been flowing together? You would probably have to be pretty powerful! Or, would you?

Materials:

- nail (8- or 16-penny)
- hammer
- soup can (empty)
- water
- masking tape

Procedure:

1. Ask an adult to use a hammer and nail to make two small holes in the lower section of the soup can. The holes should be close to the bottom and 0.5 inches (1.27 cm) apart. Tape over the holes.

2. Fill the can with water and hold it over a sink. Then, remove the tape.

3. Using your fingers, try to pinch the two streams of water together.

4. Using your fingers, try to split the two streams of water.

What's This All About?

When you pinch the streams of water together, the water molecules act like magnets. They attract each other and form larger water drops.

By splitting the water streams, you push the streams far enough away that they cannot attract each other. When this happens, they stay separate. As long as you have water in the can, you will be able to pinch or split the streams of water.

Animals Around the World

Studying animals is a great way to learn about different places in the world. Go to the library and check out books about animals that live in other parts of the world. Or, search the Internet with an adult to find out about animals. Choose an animal that lives on each continent (Africa, Antarctica, Asia, Australia, Europe, North America, and South America). As you read about each animal, you may find that the climate (weather patterns) or the food that grows in a place affects which animals live there. On the chart, write the name of each animal, the continent on which it lives, and why it lives there.

ANIMAL	CONTINENT	WHY IT LIVES THERE

BONUS

Dessert Map

A relief map shows the physical features of a place, such as rivers and mountains. Sometimes it is called a *topographical map*. You will call this a delicious map when you are finished with this activity!

Make this map in the kitchen with an adult's help. You will need two packages of prepared sugar cookie dough. You will also need some toppings, such as chocolate syrup, sliced fruit, and sprinkles.

Press the cookie dough from one package onto a cookie sheet. Use the other package of cookie dough to mold and shape land features. You could make mountains, hills, islands, volcanoes, deserts, forests, and valleys.

Bake the "map," following the directions on the package. Let the map cool. Use chocolate syrup to make water features, such as lakes and rivers. Highlight other features with different toppings.

Share the dessert with your family. Tell them what you learned about relief maps.

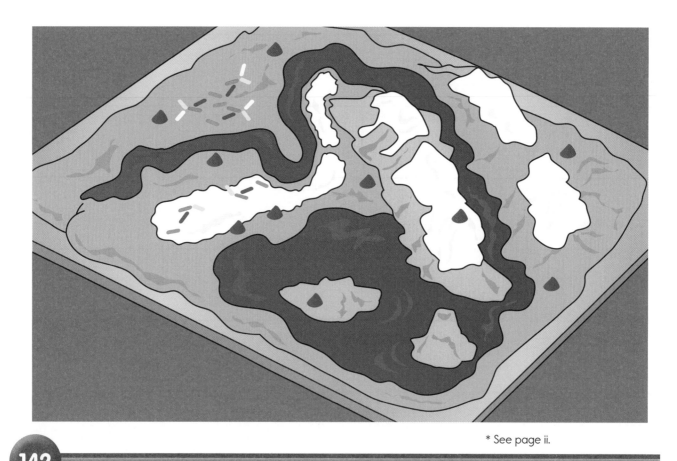

* See page ii.

Earth Effects

Earth is a big place. Did you know that what you do every day can affect the planet? Almost every human action does something to Earth. Think about this: If a family goes to the beach for the day and leaves behind a few soft drink cans, a newspaper, and an empty sunscreen bottle, they have had a negative effect on our planet. But, if they had simply taken the items with them and dropped them off in recycling bins, they would have had a positive effect on Earth. The metal cans, newspaper, and sunscreen bottle could be recycled and made into something new. Trash would not have littered the beach. The ocean animals would not have been hurt by the trash left behind.

Do you want to have a positive effect on Earth? Have your family members help you make a list of things you can do to be good to the planet.

_____

_____

_____

_____

_____

_____

_____

BONUS

Take It Outside!

Collect several different small outdoor
objects: a pinecone, a leaf, a flower, a nut,
a rock, and other safe, interesting outdoor
things. Put each item on the ground. Look at
it. Decide whether each item is symmetrical.
Symmetrical means that if you cut something
in half, the two sides will look the same and
have the same parts. If they do, then the
object is symmetrical. If they do not, then the
object is asymmetrical.

Pick up a notebook and pencil. Now, take a walk. As you go, write 10 things you see. Then,
write two words to describe each thing. This is good practice for writing adjectives and a
great way to take a look at nature.

When you are outside, list the things you see, such as the names on your neighbors'
mailboxes. Practice putting the names in ABC order. As you improve, make the list longer
to include many outside objects. Challenge yourself to find something that starts with
each letter of the alphabet. Good luck with *Q* and *X*!

* See page ii.

Section I

Day 1/Page 3: 1. sight—storm clouds moving in; 2. touch—tiny sprinkles on my face; 3. taste—little drops inside my mouth; 4. hearing—tapping a rhythm on the window; 5. smell—clean, fresh air; The capital letters should be written from A to Z.; 6. o; 7. a; 8. e; 9. u; 10. i; 11. o

Day 2/Page 5: 1. 4; 2. 12; 3. 5; 4. 18; 5. 16; 6. 20; 7. 17; 8. 8; 9. 14; 10. 18; 11. 13; 12. 19; 13. Sanja ate soup for lunch.; 14. Eli will race down the hill.; 15. Abby splashes her brother in the pool.; 16. The piano needs to be tuned.; 17. Ty slammed the car door.; The lowercase letters should be written from a to z.; 18. Drawings will vary.

Day 3/Page 7:

1. ;

2. ; 3. 6:30;

4. ; 5. 2:30;

6. ; 7. e; 8. i; 9. o;

10. a; 11. a; 12. i;

Base Word	Add -ed	Add -ing
jump	jumped	jumping
pat	patted	patting
open	opened	opening
start	started	starting
touch	touched	touching
blink	blinked	blinking

13. tape; 14. mop; 15. slide

Day 4/Page 9: 1. Students should color one-half of the rectangle.; 2. Students should color one-fourth of the circle.; 3. Students should color two-fourths of the rectangle.; 4. can; 5. pan; 6. pin; 7. cube; 8. kite; 9. cap; 10. 20; 11. 50; 12. 10; 13. 20; 14. 30; 15. 40; 16. ?; 17. ?; 18. .; 19. .; 20. ?; 21. ?; 22. !; 23. !; 24. .; 25. ?

Day 5/Page 11: 1. 5 + 8 = 13, 13 − 8 = 5, 13 − 5 = 8; 2. 5 + 7 = 12, 7 + 5 = 12, 12 − 7 = 5, 12 − 5 = 7; 3. 8 + 6 = 14, 6 + 8 = 14, 14 − 8 = 6, 14 − 6 = 8; 4. o; 5. u; 6. a; 7. e; 8. a; 9. i; 10. 4; 11. 9; 12. 9; 13. 9; 14. 6; 15. 9; 16. 4; 17. 8; 18. 9; 19. 4; 20. 6; 21. 6; 22. Students should add a comma after August 5.; 23. Students should add a comma after April 18.; 24. Students should add a comma after August 11.; 25. Students should add a comma after June 4.; 26. Students should add a comma after October 23.; 27. Students should add a comma after July 4.

Day 6/Page 13: 1. 24; 2. 40; 3. 33; 4. 57; 5. 26; 6. 45; 7. e; 8. a; 9. i; 10. e; 11. u; 12. o; 13. read; 14. angry; 15. kick; 16. watch; 17. smooth; 18. happy

Day 7/Page 15: 1. 15 train cars; 2. 8 deer; 3. 18 words; 4. 19 markers; 5. 4, 6; 6. 1, 9; 7. 8, 4; 8. 6, 4; 9. 40; 10. 11; 11. 93; 12. 28; 13. 17 flowers; 14. 18 animals; 15. 20 fruits; 16. 14 animals;

17. bow; 18. eye; 19. sun

Day 8/Page 17: 1.–14. Students should circle the number sentences for numbers 1, 2, 5, 7, 8, 10, 11, and 12.; 15.–17. Answers will vary.; 18. dark; 19. girls; 20. hop; 21. wet; Answers will vary.

Day 9/Page 19: 1. Possible answers: thick, heavy, quiet, thick, gray, blanket; 2. Xander's room and backyard; 3. Possible answer: Xander woke up. He went outside. It was a very foggy morning.; 4. D; 5. B; Answers will vary.

Day 10/Page 21: 1. 20; 2. 70; 3. 40; 4. 10; 5. doctor; 6. farmer; 7. pilot; 8. teacher; 9. baker; The following words should be colored blue: fry, tie, light, my, sigh, try, bike, sign, pie, guy, by, high, dry, bite, time, night, cry, dime, fine, lie, sight, why, right, shy, ride, buy, side, hike, kite, nine.; The following words should be colored green: bib, wig, six, if, fib, gift, pit, miss, fish, lit, chin, sit, hill, hid, bill, quit, bin, mitt, tin, win, fit, will, pin, fin, zip, did.; 10. backed, baked; 11. whent, went; 12. trane, train; 13. rom, room

Day 11/Page 23: 1. 5, 2, 3, 5; 2. 9, 2, 7, 2; 3. 8, 3, 5, 5, 3, 8, 5; 4. 4 + 3; 5. 7 + 5; 6. 6 + 9; 7. C; 8. 2, 1, 3

Day 12/Page 25: 1. 14; 2. 9; 3. 10; 4. 1; 5. 18; 6. 2; 7. dr; 8. tr; 9. gr; 10. cl; 11. gl; 12. st; 13. 19, 39; 14. 80, 100; 15. 3, 23; 16. 65, 85; 17. Ducks like to swim.; 18. Can we play in the sandbox?; 19. Some birds make nests in trees.; 20. Are you having fun today?

Day 13/Page 27: 1. Students should underline the s in stella 3 times.; 2. Students should underline the r in rodrigo 3 times.; 3. Students should underline the k in kerry and a in august 3 times.; 4. Students should underline the j in july 3 times.; Students should circle the cake, whale, gate, and grapes.; 5. Bella's balloon; 6. Kate's kite; 7. Hasaan's hat; 8. Sammy's soccer ball; 9. red; 10. blue; 11. red; 12. blue

Day 14/Page 29: 1. 9, 9, 4, 5; 2. 2, 6, 8, 6, 2, 6; 3. Answers will vary but may include: 7, 3, 10, 3, 7, 10, 10, 7, 3, 10, 3, 7;

Common Nouns	Proper Nouns
hippo	Olivia
holiday	Greenlawn Library
cousin	Dr. Yang
store	Thanksgiving

4. C; 5. B; 6. his; 7. their; 8. her; 9. my

Day 15/Page 31: 1. 12 baseballs; 2. 7 apples; Answers will vary.; 3. C; 4. 3, 1, 2

Day 16/Page 33: 1. Q; 2. E; 3. C; 4. S; 5. S; 6. and; 7. or; 8. so; 9. but; 10. The bee is on the flower.; 11. The bird is on the bowl.; 12. 2; 13. 1; 14. 1; 15. 2

Day 17/Page 35: 1. melted; 2. sweeter; 3. untie; 4. fearful; 5. reread; 6. preheat; 7. a; 8. o; 9. u; 10. a; 11. i; 12. i; 13. on top of; 14. next to; 15. under; long a: great, break, steak; long e: peach, leaf, beat

Day 18/Page 37: 1. 4, 1; 2. 4, 5; 3. 8, 4; 4. 6, 5; 5. 7, 2; 6. 1, 7; 7. 3, 9; 8. 5, 0; 9. 5, 1; 10. 9, 7; 11. 10, 0; Answers will vary.; 12. 4; 13. 2; 14. 5; 15. 3; 16. 1;

Answers and drawings will vary.

Day 19/Page 39: 1. <; 2. >; 3. <; 4. >; 5. >; 6. >; 7. >; 8. <; 9. <; 10. <; 11. >; 12. >; 13. <; 14. <; 15. >; 16. Students should draw a circle.; 17. Students should draw a triangle.; 18. Students should draw a square or a rhombus.; 19. Students should draw a square or a parallelogram.; 20. ant; 21. baby; 22. key; 23. dog

Day 20/Page 41:

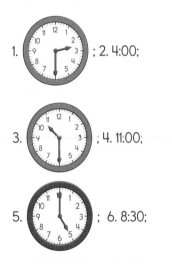

1. ___ ; 2. 4:00; 3. ___ ; 4. 11:00; 5. ___ ; 6. 8:30;

7. ch; 8. wh; 9. sh; 10. 1; 11. 3; 12. 2; 13. C; 14. A; 15. B

Section II

Day 1/Page 51: 1. 65, 80, 85; 2. 330, 360, 380; 3. 500, 600, 800; 4.–5. Answers will vary.; 6. The sun will shine today.; 7. I walked a mile today.; 8. We painted our fence.; 9. She will knit something for me.; 10. 154; 11. 90; 12. 122; 13. 75

Day 2/Page 53: 1. 71; 2. 91; 3. 72; 4. 34; 5. 41; 6. 40; 7. 99; 8. 80; 9. 54; 10. glue; 11. frog; 12. clock; 13. bowl; 14. C; 15. B; 16. it is; 17. we are; 18. you have; 19. do not; 20. we will; 21. is not

Day 3/Page 55: 1. 48¢; 2. 62¢; 3. 39¢; 4. 25¢; 5. 12; 6. 12; 7. 10; 8. 14; 9. 17; 10. 16; 11. 4; 12. 5; 13. 4; 14. 0; 15. 8; 16. 4; 17. rake; 18. tag; 19. call; 20. gate

Day 4/Page 57: 1. sipped; 2. pounded; 3. nervous; 4. exhausted; 5. 12, even; 6. 18, even; 7. 9, odd; 8. 5, odd

Long a	Long e	Long i
apron	eagle	rider
Monday	season	bedtime
flavor	fever	unkind

Long o	Long u
frozen	bugle
ocean	argue
hello	human

9. you; 10. give; 11. sit; 12. mix

Day 5/Page 59: Answers will vary.; Answers will vary.; 1. Olivia lives on a farm.; 2. Olivia wakes up early to do chores.; 3. Answers will vary but may include: Olivia feeds the horses and the chickens, collects the eggs, and helps milk the cows.; 4. Olivia's favorite thing to do in the morning is eat breakfast.; 5. oi; 6. oi; 7. oi

Day 6/Page 61: 1. 6; 2. 3; 3. 12; 4. 15; 5. 7; 6. 7; 7. 14; 8. 9; 9. 15; 10. 12; 11. 14; 12. 30;

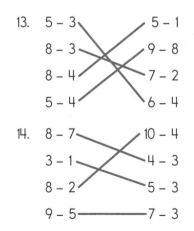

13.
5 – 3	5 – 1
8 – 3	9 – 8
8 – 4	7 – 2
5 – 4	6 – 4

14.
8 – 7	10 – 4
3 – 1	4 – 3
8 – 2	5 – 3
9 – 5	7 – 3

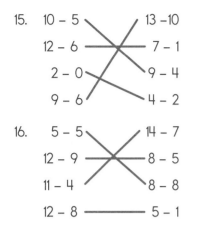

15.
10 – 5   13 –10
12 – 6   7 – 1
2 – 0   9 – 4
9 – 6   4 – 2

16.
5 – 5   14 – 7
12 – 9   8 – 5
11 – 4   8 – 8
12 – 8   5 – 1

17. gift, his; 18. car, flat; 19. sat, the; 20. dad, store

Day 7/Page 63: 1. Sidney's umbrella is old.; 2. Tabby is a farm cat.; 3. I think it will snow.; 4. 53 inches; 5. 66°; 6. 89 inches; 7. 31 pounds; 8. yes; 9. no; 10. yes; 11. e, i, e, e, i; 12. i, e, i, e, e; 13. i, i, e, e, i

Day 8/Page 65: 1. book; 2. leg; 3. cat; 4. chair; 5. apple; 6. Tom; 7. park; 8. basket; 9. oy, boy; 10. oy, toy; 11. oi, soil; 12. oi, point; 13. oy, oyster; 14. oi, voice; 15. A; 16. B; 17. He keeps practicing.

Day 9/Page 67: 1. sang; 2. ring; 3. is; 4. ran; 5. take; 6. has; Answers will vary.; 7. 28¢; 8. 25 stamps; 9. 28 fish; 10. 23 balloons; children; mice; foot; men; tooth; person

Day 10/Page 69: 1. 53; 2. 97; 3. 30; 4. 57; 5. 78; 6. 79; 7. sh; 8. th; 9. ch; 10. 8, 10, 12; 11. 8, 16, 20, 24; 12. 10, 20, 25; 13. it's; 14. they've; 15. we'll; 16. I'm; 17. you'll; 18. she'll

Day 11/Page 71: 1. Students should divide rectangle into 3 rows and 4 columns, 12.; 2. Students should divide rectangle into 4 rows and 5 columns, 20.; Answers will vary.;

Answers will vary but may include trap, pin, car, map, can, and trim.; 3. gold/fish; 4. pop/corn; 5. day/time; 6. dog/house; 7. space/ship; 8. rail/road; 9. blue/berry; 10. sail/boat; 11. grape/fruit; 12. cup/cake; 13. news/paper; 14. some/time

Day 12/Page 73: 1. 8; 2. 1; 3. 3; 4. 9; 5. 2; 6. 4; 7. 7; 8. 2; 9. 4; 10. 9; 11. 3; 12. 7; 13. 8; 14. 10; 15. 3; 16. 11; 17. 4; 18. 5; 19. 2:05; 20. 11:05; 21. 3:55; 22. 5:35; 23. 10:40; 24. 7:20; 25. 2; 26. 3; 27. 4; 28. 1

Day 13/Page 75: 1. 23; 2. 46; 3. 18; 4. 54; 5. 39; 6. 67; 7. Jonah's; 8. cat's; 9. Dante's; 10. tree's; 11. boy, shoe; 12. She, letter, aunt; 13. you, sandwich; 14. We, movie, butterflies; 15. sister, ring; January, February, March, April, May, June, July, August, September, October, November, December

Day 14/Page 77: 1. 5, 7, 3, 9, 11; 2. 1, 7, 13, 15, 17; 3. 5, 11, 9, 13, 17, 19, 3; 4. 6, 2, 4, 8, 12; 5. 8, 10, 6, 12, 16; 6. 14, 16, 12, 18, 4, 8; 7. sweet; 8. beach; 9. boat; 10. pie; 11. throw; 12. play; 13. coin; 14. toy; 15. paw; 16. daughter; Answers and drawings will vary.

Day 15/Page 79: 1. The ferrets lived in the American West.; 2. The scientists worked to save the ferrets.; 3. The number of ferrets increased after the scientists started working to save them.; 4. C; 5. B; 6. 1, 0, 1; 7. 1, 4, 3; 8. 1, 9, 11; 9. 9, 3, 2; 10. can't; 11. I'm; 12. you're; 13. don't; 14. he's; 15. I'll; 16. did not; 17. is not; 18. you have; 19. she is; 20. could not; 21. we are

Day 16/Page 81: 1. are; 2. is; 3. is; 4. are; 5. Is; 6. Are; Answers will vary.;

Answers will vary.; 7. ?; 8. !; 9. !; 10. ?; 11. .; 12. 11; 13. 12; 14. 8; 15. 14; 16. 9; 17. 6; 18. 11; 19. 7; 20. 2; 21. 11; 22. Students should underline three times the v and d in valentine's day.; 23. Students should underline three times the t and c in tasty crunch.; 24. Students should underline three times the l and d in labor day.; 25. Students should underline three times the c and n in chicken nibblers.

Day 17/Page 83: 1. B; 2. C; 3. A; 4. A; 5. 18; 6. 15; 7. 14; 8. 14; 9. 13; 10. 19; 11. 15; 12. 15; 13. 16; 14.11; 15. 11; 16. 20; 17. ourselves; 18. themselves; 19. yourself; 20. herself; 21. myself

Day 18/Page 85:

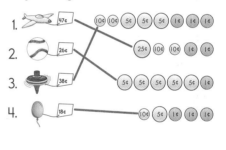

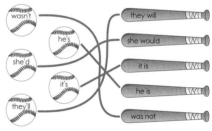

5. B; 6. A; 7. C

Day 19/Page 87: 1. oak; 2. six; 3. funny; 4. red; 5. hard; 6. furry; 7. A; 8. A; 9. Two nickels should be circled.; 10. A penny, a nickel, and a dime should be circled.; 11. Two dimes and a nickel should be circled.; 12. Four dimes and a nickel should be circled.; 13. not safe; 14.

build again; 15. not like; 16. cook before

Day 20/Page 89: 1. 6; 2. 4; 3. 4; 4. 12; 5. 10; 6. 2; 7. 5; 8. 10; 9. 19; 10. 2; 11. 14; 12. 12; 13. 13;

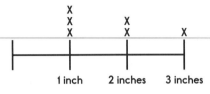

Check the drawing.; Answers will vary.

Section III

Day 1/Page 99: 1. 18, 17, 19, 13, 14; 2. 10, 14, 12, 15, 11, 13; 3. 16, 12, 14, 13, 10, 11; 4. can't; 5. easy; 6. key; 7. buy; 8. light; 9. once; 10. carry; 11. you're; 12. star; 13. funny; 14. B; 15. A; The following words should be written under *nose*: coat, drove, rope, those.; The following words should be written under *pop*: rock, fox, job, top.

Day 2/Page 101: 1. 0, 2, 5, 6, 3; 2. 7, 6, 4, 5, 3, 8; 3. 9, 5, 7, 3, 6, 4; 4. Jackson made a fruit salad, and Lena brought dessert.; 5. The bunny hopped across the yard, but the cat did not see it.; 6. I could hear the rain on the roof, so I knew the storm had begun.; 7. Julia walks to school with Chase, or she rides the bus.; 8. 9 miles; 9. 9 miles; 10. no; 11. no; 12. yes; 13. no; 14. yes; 15. no; 16. no

Day 3/Page 103: 1. 41; 2. 71; 3. 93; 4. 81; 5. 100; 6. 100; 7. 90; 8. 100; 9. 91; 10. 62; 11. 9 cm, 6 cm, 3 cm; 12. 8 cm, 4 cm, 4 cm; 13. 0 hundreds, 4 tens, 8 ones, 48; 14. 1 hundred, 4 tens, 4 ones, 144; 15. 3 hundreds, 1

ten, 5 ones, 315; 16. 8 hundreds, 3 tens, 7 ones, 837

Day 4/Page 105: 1. 996; 2. 21; 3. 82; 4. 37; 5. 265; 6. 661; 7. 79; 8. 58; 9. 22; 10. 780; 11. 118; 12. 100; 13. 46 inches; 14. 58 sunflowers; 15. 92 cans; 16. $18; 17. big—little; 18. slow—fast; 19. white—black; 20. This poem is about a missing cat.; 21. The cat is big, it has black spots, and it runs fast.

Day 5/Page 107: 1. 323; 2. 517; 3. 590; 4. 260; 5. 393; 6. 100; The following words should be written under *cow*: how, brown, clown, tower, crown.; The following words should be written under *pillow*: blow, elbow, bowl, mow, own.; 7. A; 8. E; 9. F; 10. C; 11. B; 12. D; Answers will vary.

Day 6/Page 109: 1. +2; 2. –2; 3. +10; 4. –1; Answers will vary. 5. A; 6. A philatelist is a person who collects stamps.; 7. There are different ways to find stamps.; 8. The author wrote it to explain how to collect stamps.

Day 7/Page 111: 1. 1 fourth; 2. 2 thirds; 3. 2 halves; 4. fireworks; 5. grandfather; 6. cartwheel; 7. sunflower; 8. snowflakes; 9. waterfall;
10. 20 (circled), 19, 15, 17; 11. 16, 19 (circled), 18, 12; 12. 19 (circled), 10, 13, 16; 13. 11, 14, 19 (circled), 13; 14. B, C

Day 8/Page 113: 1. about 4 in., about 11 cm; 2. about 3 in., about 9 cm; 3. wash the car; 4. $7.00; 5. $0.50; 6. N; 7. Y; 8. Y; 9. N; 10. Y; 11. N; 12. Y; 13. N

Day 9/Page 115: 1. Three-fourths of the shape should be colored.; 2. One-third of the shape should be colored.; 3. One-fourth of the shape should be colored.; 4. Two-thirds of the shape should be colored.; 5. fruit bowls; 6. 20 more fruit bowls; 7. fruit bowls; 8. 55 students; 9. 91 shells; 10. 32 laps; 11. 84 fish; 12.–14. Answers will vary.

Day 10/Page 117: 1. 6 + 7 = 13, 7 + 6 = 13, 13 – 7 = 6, 13 – 6 = 7; 2. 7 + 8 = 15, 8 + 7 = 15, 15 – 8 = 7, 15 – 7 = 8; 3. 10 + 7 = 17, 7 + 10 = 17, 17 – 10 = 7, 17 – 7 = 10; 4. 6 + 8 = 14, 8 + 6 = 14, 14 – 8 = 6, 14 – 6 = 8; 5. 7 + 5 = 12, 5 + 7 = 12, 12 – 7 = 5, 12 – 5 = 7; 6. 5 + 6 = 11, 6 + 5 = 11, 11 – 6 = 5, 11 – 5 = 6; Answers will vary.; 7. 21; 8. 3; 9. 16; 10. 6; Answers will vary.

Day 11/Page 119: 1. 4 + 4 + 4 + 4 + 4 = 20 or 5 + 5 + 5 + 5 = 20; 2. 3 + 3 + 3 + 3 = 12 or 4 + 4 + 4 = 12; 3. 6 + 6 + 6= 18 or 3 + 3 + 3 + 3 + 3 + 3 = 18; 4. 6 + 6 + 6 + 6 = 24 or 4 + 4 + 4 + 4 + 4 + 4 = 24; 5. family; 6. herd; 7. school; 8. class; 9. table; 10. square; 11. sky; 12. light

Day 12/Page 121: 1. 12:00; 2. 9:15; 3. 2:30; 4. 4:00; 5. a/part/ment; 6. e/nor/mous; 7. sub/trac/tion; 8. won/der/ful;
9. 500; 10. 900; 11. 300;
12. 1,000; 13. 800; 14. 700;
15. 1, 3; 16. 4, 35; 17. 6, 57;
18. 5, 49

Day 13/Page 123:

Kate	X	X	X	O
Grace	X	O	X	X
Jade	O	X	X	X
Meghan	X	X	O	X

Answers will vary.; 1. F; 2. F; 3. T; 4. T; 5. walk; 6. go; 7. tired; 8. full; 9. B; 10. *Aunt Antonym* is an example of alliteration because *Aunt* and *Antonym* begin with the same sound.

Day 14/Page 125: 1. 600; 2. 300; 3. 100; 4. 200; 5. 500; 6. 500; 7. 10, 12, 14, 16, 18, 20, +2; 8. 40, 50, 60, 70, 80, 90, +10; 9. 20, 25, 30, 35, 40, 45, +5; 10. 15, 18, 21, 24, 27, 30, +3; Answers will vary.

Day 15/Page 127: 1. 9; 2. 6; 3. 12; 4. 15; 5. 12; 6. 8; 7. 20; 8. 16; 9. to change from a liquid into a gas; 10. camouflage; 11. dry; 12. Possible answers: rain and snow; 13. 3, 4, 1, 300 + 40 + 1; 14. 5, 6, 3, 500 + 60 + 3; 15. 7, 5, 2, 700 + 50 + 2; 16. 8, 4, 5, 800 + 40 + 5; 17. 65; 18. 74; 19. 30

Day 16/Page 129: 1. B; 2. After you plant a seed, a tiny seedling pushes its way out.; 3. Energy comes from food.; 4. You might need to water your plant if there is little rain where you live.; 5. The word *energy* is in bold print because it is important for understanding the text.; 6. a mayor; 7. an officer; 8. a doctor; 9. a scientist; 10. an athlete; 11. an explorer; 12. an artist; 13. six; 14. hairy; 15. hard; 16. black; 17. beautiful; 18. powerful; 19. four; 20. green

Day 17/Page 131: 1. <; 2. >; 3. >; 4. <; 5. <; 6. >; 7. <; 8. <; 9. <; 10. >; 11. >; 12. <; 13. thought; 14. caterpillar; 15. cents; 16. dragon; 17. chain; 18. special; 19. O; 20. F; 21. F; 22. O; 23. O; 24. O

Day 18/Page 133: 1. C; 2. The position of the moon as viewed from Earth makes the moon's appearance change.; 3. A new moon happens when the moon is between the sun and the earth.; 4. A full moon happens when the earth is between the sun and the moon.; 5. A; 6. about 7 cm; 7. about 9 cm; 8. about 3 cm; 9. about 5 cm; 10. C; 11. They ran out of flour.

Day 19/Page 135: 1. B; 2. The author says you should take care of your teeth because teeth are important for chewing food.; 3. Baby teeth fall out and are replaced by adult teeth.; 4. 32 teeth; 5. C; 6. 23; 7. 20; 8. 25; 9. 59; 10. 28; 11. 63; 12. 27; 13. 63; 14. 67; 15. 26; 16. 29; 17. 17; 18. to take in; 19. sleepy; 20. winning; a success; 21. a rope used for catching livestock; 22. to knock or push against; 23. cloudy; 24. someone who sells things

Day 20/Page 137: 1. 3 inches; 2. 10 inches; 3. ninth; 4. 4 inches; 5. 11 inches; 6. 11 inches; 7. proudly, how; 8. yesterday, when; 9. outside, where; 10. safely, how; 11. ahead, where; 12. early, when; 13. 479; 14. 979; 15. 376; 16. 15

Find the
base word.
reading

Find the
base word.
skipped

Find the
base word.
uncover

Find the
base word.
rethink

Find the
base word.
lights

Find the
base word.
misplace

_____ + _____

_____ + _____

_____ + _____

cover

skip

read

place

light

think

gold + fish = goldfish

dragon + fly = dragonfly

tree + house = treehouse

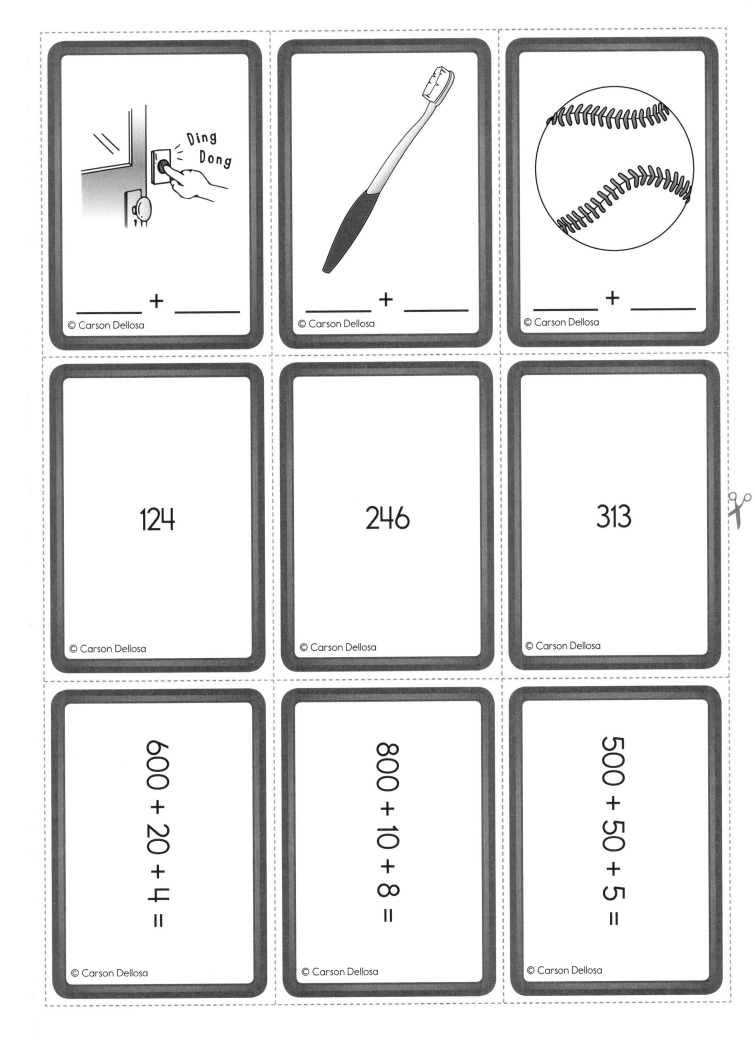

_____ + _____   _____ + _____   _____ + _____

© Carson Dellosa   © Carson Dellosa   © Carson Dellosa

124   246   313

© Carson Dellosa   © Carson Dellosa   © Carson Dellosa

600 + 20 + 4 =   800 + 10 + 8 =   500 + 50 + 5 =

© Carson Dellosa   © Carson Dellosa   © Carson Dellosa

base + ball = baseball	tooth + brush = toothbrush	door + bell = doorbell
© Carson Dellosa	© Carson Dellosa	© Carson Dellosa

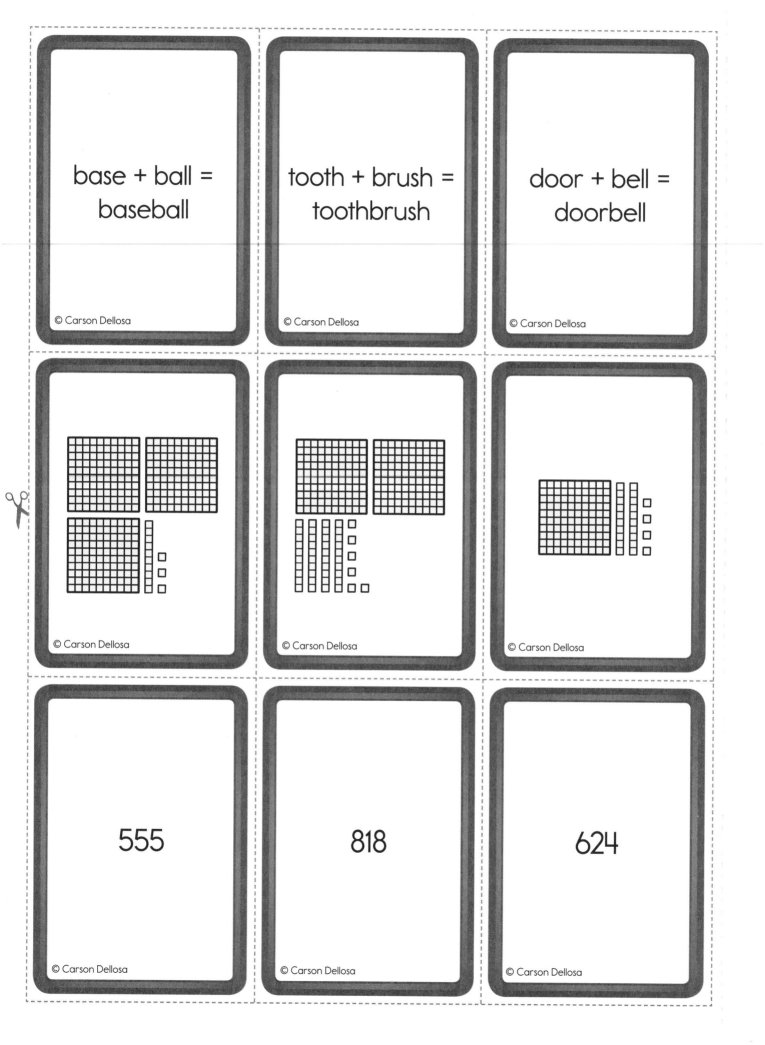

555	818	624
© Carson Dellosa	© Carson Dellosa	© Carson Dellosa

5 + 11	9 + 2	4 + 10
© Carson Dellosa	© Carson Dellosa	© Carson Dellosa
12 + 5	7 + 10	8 + 8
© Carson Dellosa	© Carson Dellosa	© Carson Dellosa
6 + 10	13 + 6	10 + 5
© Carson Dellosa	© Carson Dellosa	© Carson Dellosa

4 + 10 ―― 14	9 + 2 ―― 11	5 + 11 ―― 16
© Carson Dellosa	© Carson Dellosa	© Carson Dellosa
8 + 8 ―― 16	7 + 10 ―― 17	12 + 5 ―― 17
© Carson Dellosa	© Carson Dellosa	© Carson Dellosa
10 + 5 ―― 15	13 + 6 ―― 19	6 + 10 ―― 16
© Carson Dellosa	© Carson Dellosa	© Carson Dellosa

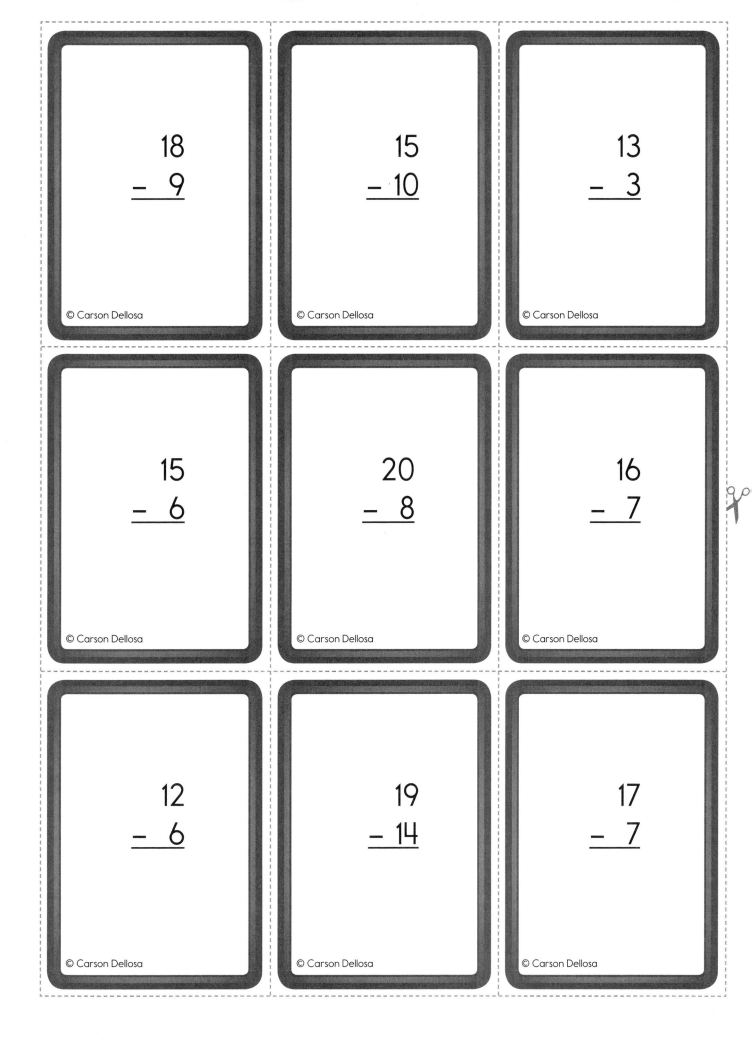

18
− 9

15
− 10

13
− 3

15
− 6

20
− 8

16
− 7

12
− 6

19
− 14

17
− 7

© Carson Dellosa

13
− 3
10

15
− 10
5

18
− 9
9

16
− 7
9

20
− 8
12

15
− 6
9

17
− 7
10

19
− 14
5

12
− 6
6

14
− 8

© Carson Dellosa

20
− 14

© Carson Dellosa

16
− 8

© Carson Dellosa

13
− 7

© Carson Dellosa

20
− 5

© Carson Dellosa

11
− 6

© Carson Dellosa

5 + 6 =

© Carson Dellosa

7 + 8 =

© Carson Dellosa

9 + 4 =

© Carson Dellosa

16
− 8
8

20
− 14
6

14
− 8
6

11
− 6
5

20
− 5
15

13
− 7
6

9 + 4 = 13

7 + 8 = 15

5 + 6 = 11

6 + 10 =	13 + 6 =	10 + 5 =
9 + 9 =	11 + 6 =	5 + 9 =
9 + 7 =	7 + 13 =	8 + 5 =

© Carson Dellosa

10 + 5 = 15	13 + 6 = 19	6 + 10 = 16
© Carson Dellosa	© Carson Dellosa	© Carson Dellosa
5 + 9 = 14	11 + 6 = 17	9 + 9 = 18
© Carson Dellosa	© Carson Dellosa	© Carson Dellosa
8 + 5 = 13	7 + 13 = 20	9 + 7 = 16
© Carson Dellosa	© Carson Dellosa	© Carson Dellosa

12 − 6 =	19 − 14 =	17 − 7 =
© Carson Dellosa	© Carson Dellosa	© Carson Dellosa
18 − 6 =	14 − 8 =	12 − 5 =
© Carson Dellosa	© Carson Dellosa	© Carson Dellosa
14 − 7 =	10 − 1 =	19 − 9 =
© Carson Dellosa	© Carson Dellosa	© Carson Dellosa

17 – 7 = 10

19 – 14 = 5

12 – 6 = 6

© Carson Dellosa

© Carson Dellosa

© Carson Dellosa

12 – 5 = 7

14 – 8 = 6

18 – 6 = 12

© Carson Dellosa

© Carson Dellosa

© Carson Dellosa

19 – 9 = 10

10 – 1 = 9

14 – 7 = 7

© Carson Dellosa

© Carson Dellosa

© Carson Dellosa

SummerBridge
ACTIVITIES

Congratulations!

This certifies that

Name

has completed **Summer Bridge Activities**.

Parent's Signature